best-ever
comfort food
recipes

best-ever
comfort food
recipes

130 mouthwatering recipes that look as good as they taste, shown in 480 stunning colour photographs

Feed the soul and heal the heart with classic, traditional and familiar recipes just like mother used to make • editor bridget jones

southwater

This edition is published by Southwater

Southwater is an imprint of Anness Publishing Ltd
Hermes House, 88–89 Blackfriars Road, London SE1 8HA
tel. 020 7401 2077; fax 020 7633 9499
www.southwaterbooks.com; www.annesspublishing.com

If you like the images in this book and would like to investigate using them for publishing, promotions or advertising, please visit our website www.practicalpictures.com for more information.

UK agent: The Manning Partnership Ltd; tel. 01225 478444;
fax 01225 478440; sales@manning-partnership.co.uk

UK distributor: Grantham Book Services Ltd; tel. 01476 541080;
fax 01476 541061; orders@gbs.tbs-ltd.co.uk

North American agent/distributor: National Book Network; tel. 301 459 3366; fax 301 429 5746; www.nbnbooks.com

Australian agent/distributor: Pan Macmillan Australia; tel. 1300 135 113;
fax 1300 135 103; customer.service@macmillan.com.au

New Zealand agent/distributor: David Bateman Ltd; tel. (09) 415 7664;
fax (09) 415 8892

Publisher: Joanna Lorenz
Editorial director: Helen Sudell
Project editor: Simona Hill
Designer: Design Principals
Production controller: Wendy Lawson

ETHICAL TRADING POLICY
At Anness Publishing we believe that business should be conducted in an ethical and ecologically sustainable way, with respect for the environment and a proper regard to the replacement of the natural resources we employ. As a publisher, we use a lot of wood pulp to make high-quality paper for printing, and that wood commonly comes from spruce trees. We are therefore currently growing more than 500,000 trees in two Scottish forest plantations near Aberdeen – Berrymoss (130 hectares/320 acres) and West Touxhill (125 hectares/305 acres). The forests we manage contain twice the number of trees employed each year in paper-making for our books.

Because of this ongoing ecological investment programme, you, as our customer, can have the pleasure and reassurance of knowing that a tree is being cultivated on your behalf to naturally replace the materials used to make the book you are holding.

Our forestry programme is run in accordance with the UK Woodland Assurance Scheme (UKWAS) and will be certified by the internationally recognized Forest Stewardship Council (FSC). The FSC is a non-government organization dedicated to promoting responsible management of the world's forests. Certification ensures forests are managed in an environmentally sustainable and socially responsible basis. For further information about this scheme, go to www.annesspublishing.com/trees

Previously published as part of a larger volume, Best-Ever Comfort Food

Front cover shows Tex-Mex Chilli Potatoes, for recipe see page 19

NOTES
• Bracketed terms are intended for American readers.
• For all recipes, quantities are given in both metric and imperial measures and, where appropriate, in standard cups and spoons. Follow one set, but not a mixture, because they are not interchangeable.
• Standard spoon and cup measures are level. 1 tsp = 5ml, 1 tbsp = 15ml,
1 cup = 250ml/8fl oz.
• American pints are 16fl oz/2 cups. American readers should use 20fl oz/2.5 cups in place of 1 pint when measuring liquids.
• Electric oven temperatures in this book are for conventional ovens. When using a fan oven, the temperature will probably need to be reduced by about 10–20°C/ 20–40°F. Since ovens vary, you should check with your manufacturer's instruction book for guidance.
• Australian standard tablespoons are 20ml. Australian readers should use 3 tsp in place of 1 tbsp for measuring small quantities of gelatine, flour, salt, etc.
• The nutritional analysis given for each recipe is calculated per portion (i.e. serving or item), unless otherwise stated. If the recipe gives a range, such as Serves 4–6, then the nutritional analysis will be for the smaller portion size, i.e. 6 servings. Measurements for sodium do not include salt added to taste.
• Medium (US large) eggs are used unless otherwise stated.

CONTENTS

INTRODUCTION

COMFORT FOOD: HAPPY MEMORIES, FAVOURITE AND FAMILIAR DISHES, EASY ENTERTAINING, PRIVATE INDULGENCES, CALM AND CONTENTMENT.

We all have our favourite comfort foods; they might be creamy, sweet, spicy, or salty, and they appeal directly to our body's feel good responses. Foods that we enjoy eating often have pleasant associations and are hard to resist. Our favourite dishes might be based on childhood memories of times when we felt safe and secure, enjoyable holidays abroad, or special celebration treats. Eating pleasurable food is deeply satisfying; it relieves us of our hunger and makes us feel content. When our hunger is satisfied after a meal that we have enjoyed, all is well with our world. We have restored our blood-sugar levels to an even balance, and our mood is restored to good humour.

Everybody likes to eat, and while not all of us like to cook, it's true that most of us are capable of rustling up the kinds of things that we do like to eat. Many favourite comfort foods are simple offerings that can be made quickly and easily: hot toast dripping with salty butter and

Above: Cheese is one of the most popular and versatile comfort foods. Enjoy it on its own, or with fruit and crackers.

flavourful, fruity jam; a thick slab of moist cake with a mug of strong coffee; a soft cheese and crunchy salad sandwich, topped with tangy pickle; or home-baked cookies dunked in a cup of tea. With ease of cooking in mind, all of the recipes in this book are no-fuss, everyday recipes, made with ingredients that are readily available. None of them

Above: Everybody has a favourite tipple, and social drinking is a comfortable and pleasant way to relax and entertain.

involve complicated cooking methods, though some do take time to cook. What they have in common is an appeal to a basic instinct in all of us. Food nurtures the body and

Below: Foods that contain carbohydrate (the pasta), protein (the meat), and fat (the melted cheese) in a single dish are nourishing and satisfying.

Below: Fatty foods, particularly those high in carbohydrates, make us feel full quickly. Carbohydrates release energy slowly, and when covered in salt, taste delicious too.

Above: Sweet and sugary foods give instant comfort. They taste good and provide an instant lift to flagging energy levels. Indisputably, home-baked cakes and cookies taste better and will keep you feeling fuller for longer than store-bought confectionery.

Above: Creamy and spicy foods can be very satisfying. The heat is uplifting, and the spiciness provides a sensory taste explosion on the palate.

nourishes the soul. Eating is essential, and we all enjoy good, flavourful food, preferably in the company of good friends or family. To that end, here is a delicious collection of 130 appealing, tried-and-tested recipes from all over the world. They taste divine, will satisfy our appetites, feed our families and make us feel good.

Comfort food does not necessarily mean unhealthy eating, although a few of these recipes might best be kept for special treats. It's really about unhurried menu planning, choosing familiar ingredients, pleasurable shopping trips and effortless food preparation. Food at its best is always home-made, and knowing it's been made using the freshest ingredients, just before it's about to be consumed, adds to our nurturing instincts. A home-cooked dish of piping hot food as we arrive

home on a cold day is a welcome pleasure; the warmth of the kitchen and the aroma of cooking both add to our emotional response to food. Likewise a warm, milky drink in the evening, before we go to bed, will make us content and sleepy. Some foods are calming and warming, while others are energy-giving, and make us feel alert and ready to face the day. For many of us, the types of food that we like to eat may be a subconscious reaction to their effect once consumed.

Enjoying food and its different aromas, tastes and textures, and learning to cook the foods that we take pleasure in eating, should be habit-forming. With so many delicious recipes at your disposal, and suitable suggestions for every meal and every possible occasion, you should never be stuck for a mealtime idea again.

Right: Sharing good food and conversation with family and friends fulfils a basic and nurturing need in us all.

THE COMFORT ZONE

Turning to food when times are tough is quite natural as our bodies recognize eating as a positive activity. Occasional indulgences are an enjoyable part of life — feel good about them and celebrate the benefits of a wide variety of comfort foods.

BEAT THE BLUES

EATING CERTAIN FOODS DEFINITELY HELPS TO LIFT THE SPIRITS. SWEET FOODS HAVE PLEASANT ASSOCIATIONS AND MEMORIES OF TREATS AND REWARDS GIVEN WHEN WE WERE LITTLE. HOMELY CARBOHYDRATE-RICH FOODS, SUCH AS TOASTED CRUMPETS OR MUFFINS, ARE AN INSTANT REMEDY.

There are plenty of reasons why we might feel at a low ebb, and at times like these, food is a good source of solace. If your mood is down temporarily, then preparing yourself a quick snack might be the answer. Low blood sugar levels produce a poor mood, so if you're feeling low because you haven't eaten recently, or haven't eaten enough of the right kinds of food, your body is sending out a clear signal.

Food is nurturing, and while a little of what we fancy does do us good, we need to make sure that what we are eating is feeding our bodies with nutrition, as well as feeding our souls.

Carbohydrates keep blood sugar levels up, and the complex starchy and wholegrain type, found in bread, rice, pasta, potatoes, fruit, pulses and legumes, help to keep blood-sugar levels steady. These foods maintain a good mood, stabilize energy levels, good concentration and they keep productivity levels up at work or school. On the other

Below: Complex carbohydrates should make up a large percentage of each meal, particularly if you are a person that feels below par on a regular basis. Choose from bread, pasta, rice, pulses, legumes, fruit and nuts, and keep stocked up with these ingredients, so that you can reach for them the moment you feel hungry.

hand, carbohydrates such as chocolate and sweet, sugary snack foods are quickly absorbed into the body giving us a short-term boost, and producing a good mood quickly. These types of treats are cheap, very appealing when we're hungry, and take no effort to prepare. The downside is that the "good mood feeling" won't last for long. For that, you need to eat a filling and healthy carbohydrate meal first and finish with a little sweet treat.

The B group vitamins are important for converting food into energy and supplying the brain with the oxygen that is important for a bright and positive outlook. They are also important for a healthy nervous system. Eating a mixed diet ensures an adequate supply of B group vitamins: meat and offal, fish, eggs, nuts and seeds, wholegrains and vegetables supply the range of vitamins that make up this group.

Vitamin C and minerals, such as magnesium, manganese and zinc, are also vital for overcoming stress and helping us to feel good and healthy. Small and frequent meals and snacks help to keep blood-sugar levels up, so

Above: Sugary foods appeal to all our senses. They look appealing, smell delicious and the taste is guaranteed to meet our expectations.

between meals reach for a piece of fruit, or a slice of toast, and keep home-made biscuits for really special treats.

Below: Canned fish is a good ingredient to keep to hand in the store cupboard. The protein that it contains helps us to stay alert.

Quick fixes

When you're feeling low, try a fast fix to help lift your spirits. Toast is a good one to start with, since cutting a thick slice of bread takes no effort and the aroma as it toasts is instantly appealing. Likewise, making a hot chocolate drink with real chocolate is extremely satisfying. If you like to bake, fill the kitchen with wafts of sweet aromas; buttery shortbread has minimal ingredients so is quickly mixed and fast to bake. Its melt-in-the-mouth taste is pure heaven.

TOPPING MUFFINS OR CRUMPETS

Freshly toasted crumpets or English muffins are reassuringly good with all sorts of toppings.

Savoury
• Spread with lots of garlic butter.
• Fill split toasted muffins with hot crisp chips (French fries), then add ketchup or mayonnaise.
• Spread with mustard, top with cheese and grill (broil) until golden.
• Top with tomatoes and bacon, then grill until aromatic and cooked.
• Top with cooked ham and a poached egg.

Sweet
• Spread with soft cheese and jam (jelly).
• Spread with peanut butter and chocolate spread.
• Pile on soft cheese and honey or maple syrup.
• Spread with unsalted (sweet) butter, chopped banana and drizzled honey.

Above: Chocolate heaven for a chocoholic.

REAL HOT CHOCOLATE

All hot milky drinks are soothing and sleep-inducing. A steaming mug of good chocolate is guaranteed to take your mind off worries and woes. Sipping the smooth, dark liquid and dunking your favourite biscuits is a tonic and a treat. You need good-quality, dark chocolate for this.

Break up 115g/4oz plain (semi-sweet) chocolate and melt it in a heatproof bowl over a pan of barely simmering water. Bring 400ml/14fl oz/ 1⅔ cups milk to the boil in a separate pan. When the chocolate has melted stir in a little of the milk, then whisk in the remainder until frothy. Pour into a mug and sweeten to taste.

Little Mexican fritters, known as churros, are the traditional accompaniment for hot frothy chocolate, but doughnuts or rich butter cookies are also delicious dunked in chocolate.

SHORTBREAD ROUNDS

These are rich, buttery and melt-in-the-mouth. They're very indulgent, but unquestionably good for the spirits. They are also easy to make, and doing a bit of baking is a good way of taking time out.

Cream 450g/1lb/2 cups butter with 225g/8oz/1 heaped cup caster (superfine) sugar until very soft and pale (a food processor is ideal for this). Sift 450g/1lb/4 cups plain (all-purpose) flour, 225g/8oz/scant 1½ cups ground rice or rice flour and 5ml/1 tsp salt together, and stir this into the creamed mixture. Pulse in a food processor to combine the ingredients. When the mixture resembles fine breadcrumbs, knead it lightly into a ball – do not overwork this dough or it will become greasy. Shape it into a long roll, measuring about 7.5cm/3in in diameter, wrap in clear film (plastic wrap) and chill until firm.

Preheat the oven to 190°C/375°F/ Gas 5. Cover two baking sheets with non-stick baking parchment. Sprinkle some demerara sugar on a piece of greaseproof (waxed) paper or baking parchment and roll the dough in this. Cut the roll into slices, about 1cm/½in thick, and place well apart on the baking sheets. Bake for 20–25 minutes, until very pale gold. Sprinkle with golden caster sugar and leave to cool for 10 minutes, until firm enough to handle. Transfer the shortbread rounds to a wire rack to cool. Makes 24.

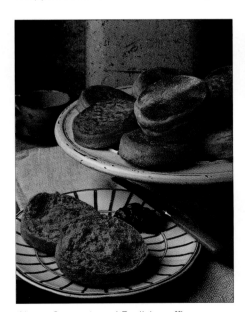

Above: Crumpets and English muffins.

Above: Churros dunked in real hot chocolate.

Above: Shortbread and tea.

TIRED OUT

When energy levels are flagging, give bought convenience foods a miss. Opt, instead, for old favourites, such as beans on toast, that are deliciously familiar and full of food value to give your body a boost.

When we're feeling exhausted and in need of instant comfort, fast fixes are the way to go. Often our response to feeling tired is to reach for high-energy foods or a drink of strong coffee in the hope that they will give us energy. Try chunky sandwiches filled with fruity jam (jelly), or mashed banana sandwiches. Both will help energy levels to rise. There are plenty of healthy and simple ideas to try that are full of nutritious ingredients yet taste delicious too.

Some foods just make you feel wide awake and full of energy. Refreshing flavours, zesty seasonings and a bit of colour work wonders. Opt for uplifting drinks to go with simple snacks or a bowl of breakfast cereal – try fresh fruit and vegetable juices, smoothies that are packed full of nutrients, and fresh fruit shakes. Use herbs and seasonings that are enlivening – sunny basil and head-clearing mint are good with savoury snacks. Fresh root ginger or pickled ginger is good in sandwiches.

When the body needs energy, go for fruit, legumes, wholemeal (whole-wheat) bread and pasta which will slowly release energy into the bloodstream, ensuring long-term recovery. This is particularly important after any form of exercise that leaves the muscles depleted of their energy supplies.

Bread and pasta, particularly wholemeal types, are good sources of complex carbohydrates. Savoury snacks on toast, such as tinned spaghetti hoops, cheese, and scrambled eggs are great

Left: Porridge and stewed fruits will give your body a good and healthy start to the day, keeping energy levels steady.

for filling you up, replacing spent energy, providing fibre and protein as well as B vitamins and minerals.

Snacks full of goodness
Being too tired to cook a proper meal should not mean missing out on balanced eating. This is the time to snack on raw food, such as fruit and vegetables that taste good just as they are. A thin slice of cheese on wholegrain crackers it is a good source of protein, calcium and B vitamins. Dried fruit and nuts are tasty and good for you; keep unsalted brazils, pecans, walnuts and hazelnuts in stock. Fruit and vegetable drinks and snacks are natural tonics that help fight tiredness and restore energy. Ideally you should satisfy hunger levels with a snack and once energy levels are back on track, cook a simple supper.

Iron is vital for the production of haemoglobin used for transporting oxygen in red blood cells. Good sources of iron include offal (variety meats), red meat, egg yolks, and dark green leafy vegetables. Vitamin C is important for iron absorption, especially to improve the availability of iron from vegetable sources.

BEANS ON TOAST
Easy and great for replenishing lost energy, especially with wholemeal (whole-wheat) breads, good old beans on toast are great on their own but can also be transformed with the addition of other ingredients.
• Toast one side of the bread, brush the other with garlic oil and grill (broil) until golden. Sprinkle with shredded basil before adding the beans.
• Mix crushed garlic, lemon zest and chopped parsley into the butter.
• Use garlic or herb bread instead of toast.

Right: This childhood favourite is great for any time of day. Thick-sliced white bread, loaded with butter and topped with hot baked beans, will fill you up and restore your energy levels.

BANANA AND PECAN SMOOTHIE

Smoothies are easy to make and drink, are full of nutrients and taste sublime. Nuts contribute vitamin E and essential fatty acids, while bananas and maple syrup provide energy. When you're too tired to cook, why not whizz up a fruit and nut smoothie?

Below: Nourishing banana and pecan smoothie.

Process 50g/2oz/½ cup pecan nuts in a food processor or blender until finely chopped. Add 2 large bananas and process to a thick paste, scraping down the nuts occasionally. Add 150ml/¼ pint/⅔ cup milk and a dollop of maple syrup and process until smooth. Pour over crushed ice and serve at once. Serves 2.

Below: Bananas are also a useful source of carbohydrate while they are still firm, before they soften and become sweet and sugary.

Above: Pecan nuts are a healthy snack, perfect to nibble at any time.

Below: A peanut butter and jelly sandwich is a nutritious childhood favourite.

PEANUT BUTTER AND JELLY SANDWICH

This traditional American snack provides sustenance, flavour and texture, and when extra fruit is added, it has extra vitamin value.

For variety, thickly slice a baguette or cut individual brioche in half to make open sandwiches. Top each half with peanut butter, jam and fresh fruit. For closed sandwiches, try light rye bread. Spread with peanut butter. Mix in some fresh fruit, such as blue-berries, blackcurrants or redcurrants; diced apple, mango or papaya; sliced strawberries; or quartered kiwi-fruit slices. Spread the fruit and jam mixture over the peanut butter. Top with more bread or serve as an open sandwich. Serve with your favourite drink. Serves 1.

UNDER ᵗʰᵉ WEATHER

SPOT THE SYMPTOMS BEFORE YOUR BODY HAS TIME TO DIP INTO ILLNESS AND USE COMFORT EATING TO FIGHT COLDS AND SIMILAR EVERYDAY ILLNESSES. THE BEST SORT OF FOOD TO GIVE THE BODY A LIFT WHEN ILLNESS THREATENS IS LIGHT AS WELL AS NURTURING AND NUTRITIOUS.

Combining comfort eating with tradition-al home cures enhances the feeling of well-being, and boosts the system to fight off mild, everyday infections. Vitamin C, found in oranges, kiwi fruit and lemons, is said to help fight off colds if taken at the first signs of symptoms.

Many herbs provide gentle remedies that are protective and help to stimulate the body's immune system. Combining natural remedies with healthy foods is a positive way to counteract feeling ill.

Small, simple and familiar

When you're feeling under the weather eating small meals regularly is the solution. When you have a poor appetite, small quantities of food can be reassuring and are more appealing than a huge meal. Simple flavours are easier on the taste buds than complex season-ings. Since our senses of taste and smell are often reduced, the appearance and texture of foods are more important. Familiar foods and basic dishes made with just a few flavourful ingredients are

Left: Manuka honey has strong antiseptic qualities, and a taste you'll appreciate if you're feeling off-colour.

more likely to arouse our interest than unusual or experimental recipes. Treats and/or childhood favourites such as mushroom omelette or boiled eggs with toast soldiers are always popular since they evoke our early memories and are very easy to eat.

Nurturing liquids

Caring for an ill person starts with providing the right hot drink. Hot toddies, with a touch of alcohol, are intended to soothe and induce sleep. Honey is a natural antiseptic and very soothing for sore throats. Lemon is often used for its vitamin C content, to help fight off infection. Ginger is an interesting ingredient – it has a warming, yet refreshing, flavour; it is also well-known for overcoming nausea and sickness. Ginger tea is easily made by infusing slices of peeled fresh root ginger in boiling water, then sweetening it with

HOME-MADE LEMONADE
This uncooked lemonade is made in minutes. It is a cooling and comforting source of vitamin C – just the drink to help fight off an irritating cold.

Mix the finely grated rind and juice of 2 lemons with 600 ml/1 pint/ 2½ cups chilled still or sparkling mineral water. Stir in 50g/2oz/¼ cup sugar until it has completely dissolved. Alternatively, add 30ml/2 tbsp honey or to taste. Serve at once. Serves 3.

Above: Fresh lemons contain vitamin C.

Above: Make fresh lemonade to feed a cold, and try it served warm in winter.

honey to taste. Milky drinks are soothing and sleep-inducing at night. Cold drinks are often welcome, particularly lemonade, which provides vitamin C.

Warming and satisfying soups are easy to eat and digest. Chicken soup is the classic choice as it is nutritious and simple in flavour. Simple vegetable soups, such as leek and potato, are usually better than any that are spicy.

Light and good

Thin bread lightly spread with butter, made into delicate sandwiches, for example with cucumber, tomato, ham or chicken, are just what's needed at times of illness and will provide comfort. Simple vegetables, such as baked or mashed potatoes, are also appealing.

Lightly grilled fish or egg dishes are nutritious, as are boiled or poached eggs, or omelettes with simple fillings. Proper custard made with eggs is nutritious. Baked egg custards are not too sweet, and they can be served with fresh fruit (such as berries or diced kiwi fruit) for added vitamin C.

Fruit makes a good snack – bananas that are not too ripe are an excellent food for a queasy stomach as they rarely cause an upset. Fruit salad made with soft fruits is a nice treat for recovery.

CHICKEN SOUP

A nutritious, flavourful chicken soup that is light on salt is best made with good stock and vegetables.

Melt a little butter in a large pan and add 2 chopped onions, 2 chopped potatoes, 1 diced carrot and 1 diced celery stick. Cook gently for 5 minutes, until the vegetables are softened slightly but not browned. Stir in 750ml/1½ pints/3 cups good chicken stock and bring to the boil. Reduce the heat, cover and simmer for 30 minutes.

Mix 25g/1oz/¼ cup plain (all-purpose) flour with 150ml/¼ pint/⅔ cup milk and stir this into the soup. Bring to the boil, stirring. Add 175g/6oz diced, cooked chicken and heat gently for 5 minutes. Finally, add 300ml/½ pint/1¼ cups single (light) cream and stir in seasoning to taste. Serve sprinkled with chopped parsley. Serves 4.

Right: Chicken soup is a traditional remedy for illness of many kinds.

HOT TODDY

A hot toddy has to be all things: soothing, calming and warming. Combine ginger to settle a swirling tummy, honey to soothe a sore throat and a tipple to lift the spirits.

Pare the rind off 2 lemons and place in a pan with 4 slices of peeled fresh root ginger, 5ml/1 tsp honey and 175ml/6fl oz/¾ cup water. Bring the ingredients to the boil, then remove from the heat and leave to infuse for 5 minutes. Stir in 175ml/6 fl oz/¾ cup Scotch whisky, Irish whiskey or American bourbon and warm through. Strain into warmed glasses. Serves 2.

Above: A hot toddy is good for colds.

MUSHROOM OMELETTE

Simple to make and easy to eat, omelettes are a good choice when your appetite has all but disappeared.

To make the filling melt 15g/1 tbsp butter and add 75g/3oz/generous 1 cup sliced mushrooms. Cook for 5 minutes. Stir in 15g/1 tbsp plain (all-purpose) flour and 85ml/3 fl oz/⅓ cup milk. Boil, stirring, and season to taste. Whisk two eggs with 15ml/1 tbsp water and seasoning. Melt a little butter in a frying pan and pour in the egg. Allow to cook, then turn and cook on the other side until browned. Turn out on to a plate and add the filling. Serves 1.

Above: Mushroom omelettes taste delicious.

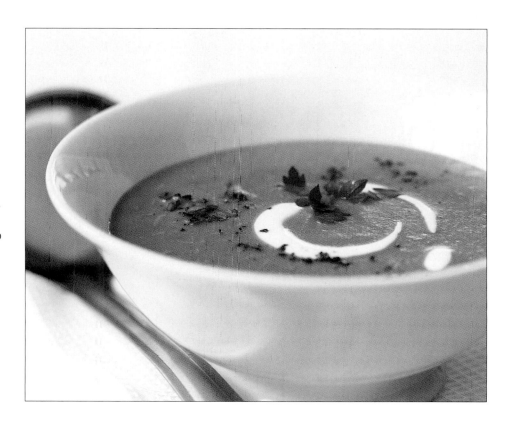

THE MORNING AFTER

HAVING A HANGOVER, THE REWARD FOR OVER-INDULGENCE, IS PROBABLY THE LEAST OF YOUR CONSIDERATIONS WHEN YOU'RE LOOKING FORWARD TO AN EVENING OUT. THE MORNING AFTER IS A DIFFERENT STORY THOUGH. FEELING TOO ILL TO FACE THE DAY? HELP IS AT HAND.

A few drinks in the company of good friends lift the spirits and provide a heady feeling that most of us enjoy. A few drinks too many, though, can have us feeling regretful the following day. This isn't a state to be endured. Food is a great healer, and there are plenty of comforting recipes that will lift the day, give you back your zing and get you back on track.

Alcohol has a severe dehydrating effect, so even though you may have drunk a lot of liquid, it will leave you feeling thirsty. Drinking water is the best cure, and lots of it. After over-indulging, the body needs a pick-me-up by way of extra B vitamins, vitamin A, C and E, plus minerals and fatty acids. So good balanced eating is essential for counteracting the effects of alcohol.

Protein foods, such as fish, meat and poultry, eggs, some dairy products, fresh fruit and vegetables, and a balance of carbohydrates are important. Most people do not feel like eating a large meal in the morning, so the breakfast – or brunch – should be welcome food that will calm the stomach, as well as the head.

Eating substantial complex carbohydrate foods, such as bread, pasta or rice, while consuming plenty of alcohol-free liquid, helps to minimize a hangover and keep the body hydrated.

Eating to feel better

Having a hangover is the classic comfort-food zone. For the worst cases, plain toast, porridge and cereals with milk are a good choice. Breakfast cereals that are fortified with B-group vitamins are good for replenishing supplies when absorption has been inhibited by alcohol. Fruit in yogurt is refreshing and nutritious – bananas are easy to digest, and low-fat yogurt with honey works wonders. Pears are light in flavour, easy to digest and not too disruptive. Papaya, mango, kiwi and orange all provide useful antioxidant vitamins.

Intense hunger often accompanies a modest hangover. A hearty cooked brunch works wonders, if eaten a few hours after waking up. Grilled tomatoes and bacon, poached or scrambled eggs, mushrooms and plenty of warm crusty bread might all appeal. If cooking is too much trouble, cooked ham or finely

sliced cheese in wholemeal rolls is plain, comforting and satisfying.

Semi-sweet breads, such as currant buns or brioche, or American muffins with fresh and dried fruit and bran are a perfect choice. Blueberry muffins are refreshing, and they go well with bananas in yogurt.

Below: Home-baked muffins are a delicious start to a hangover day.

BACON SANDWICH

A brilliant morning-after cure, bacon sandwiches provide vitamins, minerals and comforting familiarity. Use your favourite ingredients – back bacon or thin and crispy rashers (slices). Use soft or crisp rolls, or thick slices of fresh bread. The cut sides of the rolls or the bread can be toasted, if liked. Butter the rolls or bread and spread with sauce, if required, such as ketchup or brown sauce. Grill (broil) or fry the bacon to taste, allowing 4 rashers for each sandwich. Place the bacon in the rolls or between two slices of bread and serve at once.

Add red bell pepper, avocado and spring onions (scallions) for antioxidant vitamins to counteract the alcohol.

Left: Grilled bacon smells divine.

PRAIRIE OYSTER
This is an alcohol-free version of the original morning-after drink, traditionally served with a large measure of spirits. Use a perfectly fresh, free-range egg. Mix 5ml/1tsp Worcestershire sauce with 5ml/1tsp white wine vinegar and 5ml/1tsp tomato ketchup in a tall glass. Slide 1 raw egg yolk into the glass, taking care not to break it, and season with cayenne pepper. Do not stir. Down the mixture in one gulp.

Above: Hangovers are not the best start to the day, but seeking comfort in food will definitely help you start to feel better. Many foods have healing qualities, and there are plenty of simple recipes that are energy-giving.

Above and right: If swallowing a raw yolk does not appeal, mix the ingredients instead with freshly squeezed orange juice.

BLOODY MARY
The last resort in terms of health, hair of the dog is a dose of alcohol to stimulate the system and dull it at the same time. This is not the best sort of morning-after cure as far as your health goes, but as a rare fix, and for anyone with a cast-iron stomach, fruit juice laced with vodka is an option, as in a bloody Mary. Buck's fizz, sparkling white wine or champagne with freshly squeezed orange juice (half and half) is more civilized and hugely refreshing. Everyone has his or her favourite recipes for this old-fashioned hangover cure. Some put tomato ketchup in it, others add a splash of sherry.

Put a slice of lemon and 2–3 ice cubes in a tall glass. Add 5ml/1 tsp Worcestershire sauce, 5ml/1 tsp lemon juice, a pinch of celery salt, about six drops of Tabasco and six twists of pepper from a mill. Stir and fill the glass to about 4cm/1½in from the top with tomato juice, then pour in a measure of vodka. Stir well. Serves 1.

Right: For a severe hangover, starting the day with more alcohol might be the only answer.

FRIDAY NIGHT FEELING

IN ON YOUR OWN? FEELING LONELY? WANT A STRESS-FREE EVENING TO WIND DOWN FROM THE WEEK AT WORK? TIME SPENT NURTURING YOURSELF WHEN YOU'RE IN ON YOUR OWN IS TIME WELL SPENT. CHOOSE INFORMAL, EASY TO PREPARE FAST-FOOD TREATS FOR INSTANT COMFORT.

Preparing for the weekend usually means re-fuelling for a different type of activity; even if it just means catching up with the housework. Weekend menu

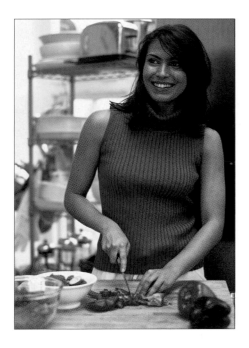

planning should cater for more relaxed cooking, and Friday evening is the night to start. Comfort cooking is about enjoying kitchen time – there's no particular rush, the recipes are familiar, favourite music brightens or calms, and the ambience is one of caring and sharing. The ingredients can be basic and may be shopped for in advance, or a brief shopping session may be part of the positive activity.

Relaxing cooking sessions should be simple. Make use of all the ready-washed and prepared ingredients:
• vegetables and salads that do not require washing, trimming and peeling
• cuts of poultry and meat that cook quickly, such as diced and stir-fry cuts or thin escalopes and steaks
• cooked meats and poultry
• fish and seafood that are cooked in

Left: Preparing the evening meal is a pleasant ritual that has a more relaxed approach at the weekend.

minutes or ready-cooked
• couscous and fresh pasta that are ready in minutes
• deli produce and good-quality canned or bottled ingredients
• breads, including long-life, part-baked breads.

Favourite and familiar

Instead of following complicated or unfamiliar recipes, preparing old favourites is fun and hassle-free. Enjoying time spent in the kitchen preparing a recipe that is tried and trusted, as well as enjoyed by all who will share it, can be a nurturing experience. Knowing you'll enjoy the finished results before the meal is even cooked makes the dinner a treat to look forward to. Best of all, the pressure is off because the results are guaranteed and while the meal cooks there is time to turn attention and thoughts to other things.

Below: Cheese risotto.

CHEESE RISOTTO

Risottos are the easiest food to prepare. They take little effort, minimal ingredients and taste absolutely delicious. Serve with wine.

Bring 1 litre/1¾ pints/4 cups beef, chicken or vegetable stock to the boil, reduce the heat so that it is simmering. Cook 1 chopped onion in 25g/1oz/2tbsp butter in a pan over gentle heat until soft and lightly browned.

Add 275g/10oz/1½ cups risotto rice and cook for 2 minutes, stirring to coat all the grains in butter. Pour in 120ml/4fl oz/½ cup dry white wine, increase the heat slightly. When the wine has evaporated, gradually add the stock, a ladleful at a time, allowing the rice to absorb each addition before adding more. After 20–30 minutes, the rice should be tender but firm and creamy.

Remove from the heat. Add a knob of butter. Stir in 75g/3oz/1 cup grated cheese and season to taste. Cover and leave to rest for 3–4 minutes. Serves 4.

HOME-MADE BURGERS AND RELISH

Easy to make and terrific to eat, these are real Friday chill-out fare. Mix 450g/1lb lean minced (ground) beef with 1 chopped shallot, 30ml/2 tbsp chopped parsley, 30ml/2 tbsp tomato ketchup and seasoning. Divide the mixture into four. Knead each portion into a ball, then flatten it into a burger.

Make a spicy relish by cooking 1 chopped shallot, 1 crushed garlic clove and 1 finely chopped and seeded green chilli in 15ml/1 tbsp olive oil for a few minutes, until softened. Add a 400g/14oz can of ratatouille and simmer for 5 minutes.

Preheat the grill (broiler) and cook the burgers for about 5 minutes on each side, until browned and cooked through. Meanwhile, split the burger buns. Arrange lettuce leaves on the bun bases, add the burgers and top with warm relish. Add the bun tops. Serve with chunky chips (French fries).

Right: Who can resist home-made burgers and relish?

TEX-MEX CHILLI POTATOES

Chilli provides heat and flavour for plain baked potatoes. This is classic comfort food to lift the spirits.

Brush 2 large potatoes with a little oil, prick, and bake at 220°C/425°F/ Gas 7 for about 30 minutes before beginning to cook the chilli.

Cook 1 chopped onion with 1 crushed garlic clove and ½ diced red (bell) pepper in a little oil for about 10 minutes, until soft but not browned. Add ½ seeded and diced small red chilli, 5ml/1 tsp ground cumin and a pinch of cayenne pepper. Stir in a 200g/7oz can tomatoes, 2.5ml/½ tsp tomato paste, 60ml/4 tbsp water and 2.5ml/½ tsp each of oregano and marjoram. Boil, reduce the heat and cover. Simmer for 25 minutes.

Add a drained 200g/7oz can kidney beans and cook, uncovered, for 5 minutes. Stir in some chopped fresh coriander (cilantro) and seasoning. Halve the potatoes, top with chilli and add a dollop of sour cream to each.

Left: Baked potatoes are great when you are weary. They don't need to be watched while they cook, and they always taste divine.

MIDNIGHT SNACKS

MUNCHING IN THE MIDDLE OF THE NIGHT BRINGS BACK MEMORIES OF CHILDHOOD ESCAPADES. LATE-NIGHT SNACKS HAVE TO BE REASSURING BECAUSE THERE ARE TIMES WHEN YOU JUST CAN'T HELP YOURSELF, BUT ALSO LIGHT SO THEY DON'T CAUSE DISCOMFORT WHEN YOU REALLY DO WANT TO SLEEP.

Midnight snacking often happens in phases, and can last for days or weeks on end. This type of snacking often goes hand-in-hand with sleeplessness, or may be a usual reaction to arriving home after a late night. When you're feeling hungry

Above: Midnight cookie binges can be pleasantly habit-forming.

SPREAD ON TOAST
When there is no time to mess about, your favourite spread on hot buttered toast is the hot option. You have to be ready for high-comfort-factor occasions – if your shopping list is non-existent, at least make sure the stock of things to spread on toast is always topped up. There should always be bread and butter in the freezer so that it can be thawed in seconds in the microwave if necessary. Slice a good loaf thickly before freezing so that individual slices can be toasted from frozen.

Spread-wise, yeast extract (such as Marmite or Vegimite) has to be top on the list. Honey, jam (jelly) or chocolate spreads work for some people, marmalade for others.

Speed is essential for things spread on toast. The butter has to be soft to spread easily; the toast thick, fresh and hot; the plate has to be warmed so that condensation does not form under the toast, giving it a soggy bottom; a hot drink must be prepared; and the whole lot has to be consumed promptly.

in the middle of the night and in need of comfort, there are some excellent recipes to test.

Raiding the food stores

All-milk drinks are calming and sleep-inducing, especially in winter. Look out for malt extract. It is similar to runny honey in texture, dark in colour and sweet with a strong malt flavour. It provides magnesium, important for the nervous system, and phosphorus. Stir a spoonful or two into a mug of hot milk.

Home-baked cookies, scones and American muffins are all deeply satisfying. Freeze some for times of need, and they can be thawed in seconds in a microwave oven. Plain muffins or those with fruit additions taste best. Chocolate is a mood-enhancing ingredient, and just a few chips in an otherwise plain recipe will do the trick, making the cake more of a treat.

Sandwich fillings and toasties

Preparing a sandwich can be a good way of diverting the mind from sleeplessness, as it requires more thought than stirring up a hot drink.

Cheese is rich and quite heavy, but it is a calming food. Chutneys and pickles that are sharp-sweet, spicy and soothing complement cheese. Dried apricots taste good with strong cheese and lettuce leaves or watercress. Toasted sandwiches are good for making a comparatively small amount of cheese go a long way.

Bananas, chocolate spread, jam and honey are all comforting foods to sandwich between substantial slices of crusty bread. Fruit buns and teabreads are good plain, but better with butter.

For grand-scale indulgence plain vanilla ice cream sandwiched between your favourite chocolate cookies makes a feast for the midnight hour.

Left: Marmite on toast. You either love it or hate it.

Below left: A scone topped with a dollop of home-made fruity jam (jelly) and a trickle of cream is the best midnight treat.

Below: Ice cream eaten straight from the tub always feels decadent, but if you can leave the ice cream to soften slightly, you'll get all the benefit of the creamy flavour, it'll taste even better.

CHEESE AND PICKLE SANDWICH

Old-fashioned cheese and pickle sandwiches always satisfy hunger pangs. This is the door-step sandwich zone: bread must be fresh and hunky; crusts are de rigueur.

Bring basic pickle to life by adding a little chopped fresh fruit – pear, apple, banana, mango or peach – with a good squeeze of lemon or lime juice. Ready-to-eat dried fruits are good; try apricots, pineapple, mango or peach. Diced red or green (bell) peppers and chopped spring onion (scallion) also pep up a standard pickle.

Cheddar and similar hard cheeses are traditional, but you could try others: Jarlsberg or Gruyère with tangy, spicy pickle; Danish Blue or Stilton for a punchy flavour; or ripe Brie for a rich and creamy taste.

Left: The ultimate cheese and pickle sandwich.

LATE-NIGHT COOKIE STACK

These are dangerous cookies. Take a pile of them to bed and all that will be left next morning will be crumbs in the sheets. Stack them with ice cream for the ultimate treat.

Preheat the oven to 180°C/350°F/ Gas 4 and grease two baking sheets. Cream 75g/3oz/6 tbsp butter with 75g/3oz/6 tbsp golden caster (superfine) sugar and 75g/3oz/6 tbsp soft light brown sugar until pale and fluffy. Beat in 1 large (US extra large) egg and 2.5ml/ ½ tsp vanilla extract. Sift 150g/5oz/1¼ cups self-raising (self-rising) flour, 25g/1oz/¼ cup unsweetened cocoa powder and 1.5ml/¼ tsp salt over the mixture. Add 100g/4oz/4 squares chopped chocolate (or chocolate chips) and fold the dry ingredients into the creamed mixture.

Place four heaped tablespoons of the mixture well apart on each baking sheet. Spread the mixture with the back of a wetted spoon and bake for 12 minutes, until risen and set. Leave on the sheets for a minute to firm up, then cool on a wire rack. Repeat with the remaining mixture. Makes 12 large or 20 small cookies.

Right: Not for the faint-hearted, this sweet concoction will satisfy all hunger pangs.

BACK FROM SCHOOL

FOND MEMORIES OF TEA~TIME TREATS THAT WERE READY TO GREET US WHEN WE ARRIVED HOME FROM SCHOOL PROVIDE A STORE OF COMFORT FOOD FOR LIFE. DELICIOUS SMALL~SCALE SNACKS THAT ARE VISUALLY APPEALING AS WELL AS FILLING ARE GUARANTEED TO BE DEMOLISHED IN AN INSTANT.

Sandwiches are nutritious, but it's really the filling that makes them appealing. Bread, preferably wholemeal (whole-wheat) or at least containing some whole grains, provides complex carbohydrates for long-term energy. Pitta breads, French breads, crusty country loaves, soda bread, rolls, bagels and fruit breads are all made for filling.

Salad vegetables are ideal for savoury sandwiches – cucumber, tomato, spring onion (scallion) and grated carrot are delicious with medium- or low-fat soft white (farmer's) cheese. Canned fish, such as sardines, salmon or tuna, are good with salad vegetables or on their own. Egg sandwiches are a real favourite and so simple – hard boiled, chopped and mixed eggs go well with sliced tomatoes or salad cress. Adding mayonnaise masks the filling's flavour – spreading generously with butter is better.

Sweet fillings comfort as well as taste moreish. Bananas go well with jam (jelly), honey or chocolate spread. Diced fresh fruit or small whole berries can be stirred into jam for added nutritional value. Nut butters provide protein and good fat; read the labels to avoid products that have a high salt content and contain hydrogenated oils or palm oil, which is high in saturated fat.

Make 'n' bake

Home-baking is an all-round comforter, making the cook feel as good as those who share the results. Make baking a family activity and all the cooks can share the results. Children love cooking, and making cakes or rolling dough is fun.

While some bought cakes and biscuits (cookies) are made with large quantities of sugar, hydrogenated oils, colouring and flavouring, home-made goodies can be full of ingredients that make a valuable contribution to the diet. Using butter makes the biscuits and cakes taste divine and adds that melt-in-the-mouth flavour. Nuts, dried and fresh fruit, and even vegetables can be used in cake recipes.

Above: Sweet treats are better when they're home-made.

Home-baked products freeze well and small portions can be removed as required, so a whole batch of cakes or biscuits does not have to be consumed in one sitting. Small cakes or slices of larger cakes thaw quite quickly at room temperature or in seconds in a microwave oven. Slice large cakes before freezing them and interleave the slices with pieces of freezer film or non-stick baking parchment.

Sweet treats

There are so many dessert treats that are fun to make and have a high nutritional value as well as satisfying every sweet tooth.

Fruit jellies can be made very simply by dissolving gelatine in fruit juice. Pour this over small fresh berries or diced fruit in individual bowls, cover and set in the refrigerator. The result is a treat that also provides a portion of fruit.

Milk-based desserts are fun to make and nutritious, and many are just right for afternoon tea. Pancakes are brilliant for sharing – both cooking and eating – and for teaching children how to prepare food and use the stove. Custards are not too sweet, and they can be served with fruit to follow sandwiches for a well-balanced light meal.

Above: Promoting an interest in food from an early age creates tomorrow's cooks.

JAM SANDWICHES

Make these nutritious as well as irresistible – it's a great opportunity for introducing a grainy bread, either wholemeal or a malted loaf with whole grains. Cut the bread thick or use rolls. Spread with soft cheese (try medium or low fat) and top with jam. Add sliced banana for food value and flavour before topping with the second slice.

Below: Jam (jelly) sandwiches are simple to make. They taste better with fresh fruit added. Try chopped banana.

JAMMY SWEETHEARTS

Process 225g/8oz/2 cups plain (all-purpose) flour and 175g/6oz/¾ cup butter in a food processor until the mixture resembles fine breadcrumbs. Add 130g/4½oz/⅔ cup caster (superfine) sugar and 1 egg yolk and pulse to combine the ingredients. Turn the mixture out on to a floured surface and knead until smooth. Shape into a ball and wrap in cling film (plastic wrap), then chill for 30 minutes.

Preheat the oven to 180°C/350°F/ Gas 4. Roll out the dough thinly and cut out 6cm/2½in rounds. Place half the rounds on greased baking sheets. Use a small heart-shaped cutter, about 2cm/¾in in diameter, to cut out the centres of the remaining rounds and place on baking sheets. Bake for about 12 minutes, until pale golden, then cool on a wire rack.

Beat 50g/2oz/¼ cup unsalted (sweet) butter and 90g/3½oz/scant 1 cup icing (confectioners') sugar together until creamy. Add a few drops of vanilla extract if you like. Sandwich the plain and cut-out biscuits together with the buttercream and fill the cut-outs with a little jam. Makes 20.

Right: Jammy sweethearts.

HOT BUTTERED PANCAKES

Sift 300g/11oz/2¾ cups plain (all-purpose) flour with 5ml/1 tsp each of bicarbonate of soda (baking soda) and cream of tartar. Stir in 75g/3oz/6 tbsp caster (superfine) sugar and make a well in the middle. Add 2 beaten eggs and 5ml/1 tsp lemon juice, then gradually beat in 400ml/14fl oz/1⅔ cups milk. Beat the dry ingredients with the eggs, adding the milk little by little to make a smooth, thick batter. Do not add all the milk until the batter is smooth, then add enough milk to make a batter the consistency of double (heavy) cream. Leave to stand for 30 minutes.

Heat a griddle pan and grease it lightly with butter. Drop spoonfuls of the batter on the griddle, leaving space between them, and cook until they are just set, bubbling on the surface and golden underneath. Turn and cook the second side. Transfer to a plate covered with a dish towel and keep warm until all the batter is cooked. Adjust the heat under the pan so that it does not become too hot and brown the outside of the pancakes before the batter is set and bubbly. Serve the pancakes hot with butter – a little jam, honey or maple syrup can be added. Serves 4.

Left: Frying pancakes have a delicious aroma.
Right: Pancakes dripping with butter.

A FRIEND IN NEED

RECIPES THAT HELP MAKE YOU FEEL CONTENT AND FULL, ARE EASY TO EAT AS WELL AS FAMILIAR ARE GOOD CHOICES WHEN IT COMES TO SPENDING TIME WITH FRIENDS IN NEED. EVERYONE APPRECIATES DELICIOUS-TASTING SIMPLE FOODS.

Simple savoury foods that are full of flavour are good to share. Everyone loves fast food, it's tasty and full of energy, but the great thing about home-made versions is that they are usually more filling meals.

Pouring out problems is the ideal excuse for sharing a plate of fries, with ketchup and mayo or any other favourite dip. Hot dogs and pizza are in the same category. Fillings and toppings must be punchy – spicy salami or chorizo, big meaty frankfurters, lots of garlic, plenty of herbs. Some breakfast favourites also work well on shared platters. Try good sausages grilled (broiled) until golden and served with a tomato chutney or salsa to dip, or grilled bacon with a stack of American-style thick pancakes and maple syrup to drizzle over them. Mini meatballs are good with garlic-laden cucumber and yogurt dip (with a hint of mint).

If inspiration is lacking and time short, bread and cheese is calming and good for sharing. Long crusty French baguettes, heated and aromatic, with big wedges of blue cheese and creamy ripe Brie can be accompanied by little cornichons, wedges of sharp-sweet apple and crunchy pickled onions.

Friendly encounters

Meeting for afternoon tea can be a treat, and an opportunity for a good chat. Cucumber sandwiches on wholemeal (whole-wheat) bread, or finger rolls filled with smoked ham, go well with afternoon tea; toasted tea cakes or English muffins are ideal. Afternoon tea will sustain you until an evening meal and because the food is light you can justify having a sweet treat. Danish pastries or a jam (jelly) and cream sponge will round off the afternoon. Jam tarts are a treat, and are extremely good topped with cream.

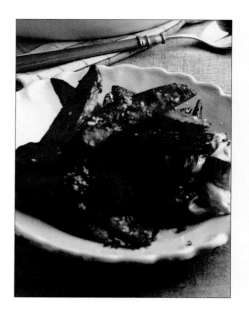

Above: A plate of fries, with salt and vinegar shaken over it, is an instant pick-me-up that's hard to resist. Eat them when they're piping hot and freshly cooked for the best taste.

CREAM TEA

Fresh scones with thick cream and fruity jam are the perfect accompaniment for a refreshing drink of tea.

Preheat the oven to 230°C/450°F/ Gas 8. Rub 50g/2oz/¼ cup diced butter into 450 g/1lb/4 cups self-raising (self-rising) flour with a pinch of salt added. Stir 15ml/1 tbsp lemon juice into 400ml/14fl oz/1⅔ cups milk and leave to stand for a minute, then stir this into the dry mixture to make a soft but manageable dough. Knead the dough lightly into a ball on a well-floured surface, then roll it out to 2.5cm/1in thick. Use a 5cm/2in cutter to stamp out rounds and place them on a greased baking sheet. Brush with a little milk and bake for about 20 minutes, until risen and golden brown. Cool on a wire rack.

Serve the scones with butter, jam and clotted cream or whipped double (heavy) cream. Makes about 12.

Left: A cream tea with jam (jelly) and cream is a quintessentially English tradition.

HOT DOGS

Fry ½ of a sliced onion for each hot dog in a little oil or butter until soft and lightly browned. Poach or grill (broil) frank-furters, 1 per bread roll, for 3–5 minutes, until they are thoroughly reheated (they are ready-cooked). Split and toast hot dog buns and spread with mustard and/or ketchup or relish. Add the frank-furters and onions and serve at once.

Update the basic hot dog by adding grilled spring onions (scallions) or thinly sliced raw onion (red for a mild flavour) instead of fried onions, with some shredded sage, mint, oregano or marjoram. Sliced tomato and peppery watercress are good. Sliced avocado is deliciously creamy with smoky frank-furters. Instead of toasted hot dog rolls, use a warm crusty baguette, flat breads, such as pitta, naan or chapati, or wraps.

Left: Hot dogs are classic American street food.

Below: The Italian love of pizza is shared the world over.

BRESAOLA AND ROCKET PIZZA

With a punchy topping, home-made pizza tastes much better than the bought alternatives, and it does not have to involve hours of hard labour.

Preheat the oven to 200°C/400°F/ Gas 6. Make up a 150g/5oz packet pizza base mix according to the instructions – usually adding about 120ml/4 fl oz/½ cup lukewarm water and kneading for 5–10 minutes, until the dough is smooth and elastic. Divide the dough in half and roll each piece out into a 23cm/9in round. Place on baking sheets.

Cook 225g/8oz/3¼ cups sliced mixed wild mushrooms in a little butter with 2 chopped garlic cloves for about 5 minutes over high heat, until the mushrooms are softened but not over-cooked. Spread the pizza bases with pesto – about 30ml/2 tbsp on each – and top each with 4 slices bresaola and 2 sliced tomatoes, placed around their edges. Spoon the mushrooms into the middle. Divide 75g/3oz/⅓ cup cream cheese between the pizzas, dotting it over the topping. Bake for 15–18 minutes. Sprinkle with rocket (arugula) and serve. Serves 4.

SPOIL YOURSELF

COMFORT EATING SHOULD BE PART OF EVERY WEEK. LUXURIOUS TREATS ARE IDEAL FOR DAYS OFF, WHEN YOU HAVE ONLY YOURSELF TO PLEASE. AFTER ALL, THE CHANCE TO NURTURE YOURSELF IS AN INVESTMENT IN YOUR WELL-BEING.

Cooking for yourself is all about pandering to your own palate, particularly so if your usual routine is to cook for a busy family. Choosing foods that you adore and tailoring a menu just for yourself can feel quite liberating, so make the most of time spent alone and catering for yourself.

This is the time to make your favourite dish, whether it's something really simple to create, such as a smoked salmon and cream cheese bagel with a glass of chilled wine, a simple snack such as corn chips with guacamole, or something that requires more complicated cooking skills and ingredients. Since eating your favourite foods is about nurturing yourself, make time to enjoy a leisurely meal without distractions. Listening to relaxing music, or eating outside in the garden on a warm day may contribute to the unhurried pace and ambience.

Quality not quantity

Choose the finest-quality ingredients that you can afford, rather than opting for quantity. The following are a few suggestions for simple treats that can be assembled from quality ingredients.
• Smoked halibut with crème fraiche on warm blini
• Gravadlax with light rye bread
• Smoked duck or venison with grated raw celeriac tossed with olive oil and snipped chives, served with warm crusty bread
• Salad of cooked asparagus drizzled with a little olive oil and lemon juice and served with the best mayonnaise, and thin bread with butter
• Smoked ham or pork with diced beetroot (beets) drizzled with honey, cider vinegar and walnut oil, served with good whole-meal walnut bread.
Choose an appropriate wine to serve with your treat and enjoy.

Above: What could be more of a treat than a glass of red wine?

CORN CHIPS WITH SALSA AND GUACAMOLE

Dice 4 seeded tomatoes and mix with 30ml/2 tbsp chopped fresh basil, the juice of ½ lime, 20ml/2 tsp good-quality sweet chilli sauce, 1 finely chopped small red onion, salt and freshly ground black pepper. Cover and leave to marinate for 1–2 hours.

For guacamole, mash the flesh from 4 ripe avocados with the juice of ½ lime and 1 seeded and diced mild green chilli. Add salt and pepper to taste. If you like, add some chopped spring onions (scallions) or diced tomato.

Brush 8 yellow corn tortillas (about 300g/11oz) with a mixture of chilli and sunflower oil on both sides, stacking them up as you do so. Cut the stack into 6 wedges. Place on a grill (broiler) pan and toast under a hot grill for about 30 seconds on each side, until browned.

Place the corn chips in bowls and leave to cool. Serve with the salsa and guacamole. Serves 4.

Right: Dips and salsas are summer treats.

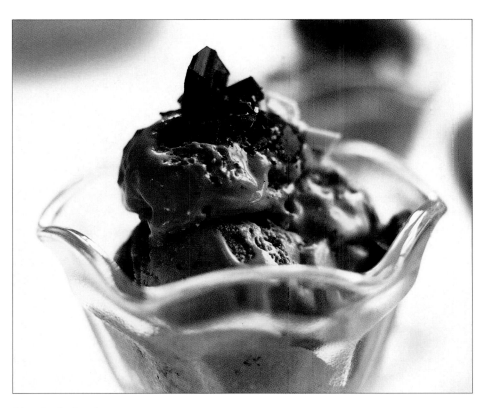

CHUNKY CHOCOLATE ICE CREAM

Whisk 4 egg yolks with 75g/3oz/6 tbsp caster (superfine) sugar and 5ml/1 tsp cornflour (cornstarch) until thick and foamy. Heat 300ml/½ pint/1¼ cups milk until just about to boil, then pour it into the egg mixture, stirring all the time. Pour this custard back into the pan and cook over a gentle heat, stirring, until thickened. Remove from the heat.

Break 150g/5oz/5 squares chocolate into pieces and stir them into the custard. When melted, cover, leave to cool, then chill. Whip 300ml/½ pint/1¼ cups whipping cream until thick, then fold it into the chocolate custard. Freeze the mixture in an ice-cream churn or in an appropriate container. If choosing a container, whisk the mixture twice during freezing. Fold in 50g/2oz/2 squares each of chopped dark, white and milk chocolate after whisking for the last time and freeze until firm. Serve decorated with chocolate. Serves 4.

Left: Delicious chunky chocolate ice cream.

Simple is best

Ripe fruit is simple, colourful and succulent. Serve it with rich Greek (US strained plain) yogurt or other full fat (whole) milk yogurt, clotted or whipped cream or crème fraiche. Select the best dessert cookies, or indulgent chocolate cookies as accompaniments. Pour small glasses of chilled dessert wine to sip with sweet dishes.

• Serve papaya and mango with wedges of lime
• Sprinkle strawberries with a little caster (superfine) sugar and kirsch
• Serve perfect strawberries or ripe figs with freshly ground black pepper
• Soak ready-to-eat dried fruit, such as apricots, figs and peaches, in brandy overnight, then drain them before serving with mascarpone. Reserve the brandy as a liqueur
• Whip double (heavy) cream with chocolate liqueur and serve as a dip for strawberries; use orange liqueur and serve the fruit with fresh apricot halves
• Serve vanilla ice cream with grated lime zest and freshly grated nutmeg.

Round off with a few good-quality chocolates and make your favourite blend of coffee.

Right: Lox and cream cheese bagels.

SMOKED SALMON AND CREAM CHEESE

Preheat the oven to 200°C/400°F/ Gas 6 and warm 2 bagels for 4–5 minutes. Slice them in half horizontally and spread generously with cream cheese. Top with smoked salmon – about 150g/5oz for both – and season with black pepper. Serve with lemon wedges. Serves 2.

BREAKFAST TO BRUNCH

There are times when a slice of toast, a banana
or cereal is all you have time for first thing in
the morning. Weekends and holidays are the time
to indulge in extravagant and lazy breakfasts.
This is a chapter full of wonderful ideas for
memorable breakfast events, from flaky morning
pastries to fabulous fry-ups.

DANISH PASTRIES

*EVEN THOUGH THESE WORLD-FAMOUS PASTRIES ARE TIME-CONSUMING TO MAKE, THE PROCESS IS
ENJOYABLE AND THE RESULTS ARE INCOMPARABLY WONDERFUL, ESPECIALLY WITH THE COFFEE FILLING.*

MAKES SIXTEEN

INGREDIENTS
   45ml/3 tbsp near-boiling water
   30ml/2 tbsp ground coffee
   40g/1½oz/3 tbsp butter
   115g/4oz/½ cup caster
      (superfine) sugar
   1 egg yolk
   115g/4oz/1 cup ground almonds
   1 egg, beaten
   275g/10oz/1 cup apricot jam (jelly)
   30ml/2 tbsp water
   175g/6oz/1½ cups icing
      (confectioners') sugar
   50g/2oz/½ cup flaked (sliced)
      almonds, toasted
   50g/2oz/¼ cup glacé
      (candied) cherries
For the pastry
   275g/10oz/2½ cups plain
      (all-purpose) flour
   1.5ml/¼ tsp salt
   15g/½oz/1 tbsp caster
      (superfine) sugar
   225g/8oz/1 cup butter, softened
   10ml/2 tsp easy-blend (rapid-rise)
      dried yeast
   1 egg, beaten
   100ml/3½fl oz/scant ½ cup chilled
      water

1 To make the pastry, sift the flour, salt and sugar into a bowl. Rub in 25g/1oz/ 2 tbsp butter. Stir in the yeast. In a separate bowl, mix the egg and water together, add to the flour mixture and mix to a soft dough. Lightly knead for 4–5 minutes. Place in a plastic bag, seal and chill for 15 minutes.

2 Put the remaining butter for the pastry between two sheets of baking parchment and beat with a rolling pin to make an 18cm/7in square. Chill.

3 Roll out the dough on a floured surface to a 25cm/10in square. Put the butter in the middle of the dough square, angled like a diamond, then bring up each corner of the dough to enclose it fully.

4 Roll out the pastry thinly to measure about 35cm/14in in length. Turn up the bottom third of the pastry, then gently fold down the top third. Seal the edges together with a rolling pin. Wrap the pastry in clear film (plastic wrap) and chill for 15 minutes.

5 Repeat the rolling and folding three more times, turning the pastry after folding over so that the short ends are at the top and bottom. Allow the pastry a 15-minute rest between each turn.

6 To make the filling, pour the hot water over the coffee and infuse for 4 minutes. Strain through a fine sieve. Cream the butter and sugar together. Beat in the egg yolk, ground almonds and 15ml/1 tbsp of the coffee.

7 Divide the dough and filling equally into three. Roll one dough portion to an 18 × 35cm/7 × 14in rectangle. Spread with filling and roll up from a short end. Cut into six equal slices. Roll another portion into a 25cm/10in round, and cut into six equal segments.

8 Put a spoonful of filling at the widest end of each segment. Roll the pastry towards its point to form a crescent.

9 Roll out the remaining dough into a 20cm/8in square; cut into four. Place some filling in the centre of each piece, and shape by making cuts from each corner almost to the centre, then fold four alternate points to the centre.

10 Preheat the oven to 220°C/425°F/ Gas 7. Space the pastries well apart on greased baking sheets. Cover loosely with oiled clear film and leave to rise for about 20 minutes, until almost doubled in size. Brush with the egg and bake for 15–20 minutes until lightly browned and crisp. Cool on wire racks.

11 Put the jam in a pan with the water; bring to the boil, then sieve. Brush the jam over the warm pastries. Mix the icing sugar with the remaining coffee to make a thick icing. Drizzle the icing over some of the pastries and decorate some with almonds or chopped glacé cherries. Leave to set before serving.

Energy 387Kcal/1623kJ; Protein 5.1g; Carbohydrate 48.1g, of which sugars 34.6g; Fat 20.8g, of which saturates 9.4g; Cholesterol 76mg; Calcium 65mg; Fibre 1.3g; Sodium 161mg.

CROISSANTS

PERFECT CROISSANTS CONSIST OF PUFFED AND FLAKY LAYERS OF YEAST DOUGH. THEIR PREPARATION, WHICH IS A SOOTHING, CREATIVE PROCESS, IS NOT TO BE RUSHED; EATING THEM IS BREAKFAST BLISS.

MAKES FOURTEEN

INGREDIENTS
  350g/12oz/3 cups (strong) unbleached white bread flour
  115g/4oz/1 cup fine plain (all-purpose) flour, preferably French
  5ml/1 tsp salt
  25g/1oz/2 tbsp caster (superfine) sugar
  15g/½oz fresh yeast
  225ml/scant 8fl oz/scant 1 cup lukewarm milk
  1 egg, lightly beaten
  225g/8oz/1 cup butter
For the glaze
  1 egg yolk
  15ml/1 tbsp milk

COOK'S TIP
Make sure that the block of butter and the dough are about the same temperature when combining, to ensure the best results.

VARIATION
To make chocolate-filled croissants, place a small square of milk or plain (semisweet) chocolate or 15ml/1 tbsp coarsely chopped chocolate at the wide end of each triangle before rolling up as in step 8.

1 Sift the flours and salt together into a large bowl. Stir in the sugar. Make a well in the centre. Cream the yeast with 45ml/3 tbsp of the milk, then stir in the remainder. Add the yeast mixture to the centre of the flour, then add the egg and gradually beat in the flour until it forms a dough.

2 Turn out on to a lightly floured surface and knead for 3–4 minutes. Place in a large lightly oiled bowl, cover with lightly oiled clear film (plastic wrap) and leave in a warm place, for about 45–60 minutes, or until doubled in bulk.

3 Knock back (punch down), re-cover and chill for 1 hour. Meanwhile, flatten the butter into a block about 2cm/¾in thick. Knock back the dough and turn out on to a lightly floured surface. Roll out into a rough 25cm/10in square, rolling the edges thinner than the centre.

4 Place the block of butter diagonally in the centre and fold the corners of the dough over the butter like an envelope, tucking in the edges to completely enclose the butter.

5 Roll the dough into a rectangle about 2cm/¾in thick and approximately twice as long as it is wide. Fold the bottom third up and the top third down and seal the edges with a rolling pin. Wrap the dough in clear film and chill for about 20 minutes.

6 Repeat the rolling, folding and chilling twice more, turning the dough by 90 degrees each time. Roll out on a floured surface into a 63 x 33cm/25 x 13in rectangle; trim the edges to leave a 60 x 30cm/24 x 12in rectangle. Cut in half lengthways. Cut crossways into 14 equal triangles with 15cm/6in bases.

7 Place the dough triangles on two baking sheets, cover with clear film and chill for 10 minutes.

8 To shape the croissants, place each one with the wide end at the top, hold each side and pull gently to stretch the top of the triangle a little, then roll towards the point, finishing with the pointed end tucked underneath. Curve the ends towards the pointed end to make a crescent. Place on two baking sheets, spaced well apart.

9 Mix together the egg yolk and milk for the glaze. Lightly brush a little glaze over the croissants, avoiding the cut edges of the dough. Cover the croissants loosely with lightly oiled clear film and leave to rise, in a warm place, for about 30 minutes, or until they are nearly doubled in size.

10 Meanwhile, preheat the oven to 220°C/425°F/Gas 7. Brush the croissants with the remaining glaze and bake for 15–20 minutes, or until crisp and golden. Transfer to a wire rack and leave to cool. The croissants are best warm, with butter, if liked, and good quality fruit conserve.

Energy 253Kcal/1059kJ; Protein 4.3g; Carbohydrate 28.5g, of which sugars 3.2g; Fat 14.4g, of which saturates 8.7g; Cholesterol 50mg; Calcium 72mg; Fibre 1g; Sodium 251mg.

AMERICAN PANCAKES <u>WITH</u> GRILLED BACON

THESE SMALL, THICK, BUTTERY PANCAKES WILL BE EATEN IN SECONDS, SO MAKE PLENTY. THE BATTER CAN BE MADE THE NIGHT BEFORE, READY FOR BREAKFAST ... OR A LATE-NIGHT SNACK ATTACK.

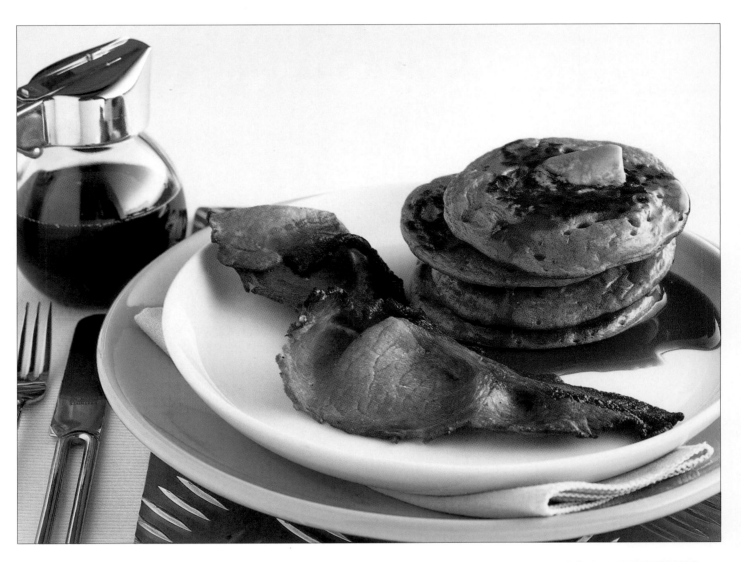

MAKES ABOUT TWENTY

INGREDIENTS
    175g/6oz/1½ cups plain (all-purpose)
      flour, sifted
    pinch of salt
    15ml/1 tbsp caster (superfine) sugar
    2 large (US extra large) eggs
    150ml/¼ pint/⅔ cup milk
    5ml/1 tsp bicarbonate of soda
      (baking soda)
    10ml/2 tsp cream of tartar
    oil, for cooking
    butter
    maple syrup
    crisply grilled (broiled) bacon, to serve

1 To make the batter, mix together the flour, salt and sugar. In a separate bowl, beat the eggs and milk together, then gradually stir into the flour, beating to a smooth, thick consistency. Add the bicarbonate of soda and cream of tartar, mix well, then cover and chill until ready to cook.

2 When you are ready to cook the pancakes, beat the batter again. Heat a little oil in a heavy frying pan or griddle. Drop dessertspoonfuls of the mixture into the pan, spaced well apart, and cook over a fairly high heat until bubbles appear on the surface of the pancakes and the undersides become golden brown.

3 Carefully turn the pancakes over with a palette knife or fish slice (metal spatula) and cook briefly until golden underneath, then transfer them to a heated serving dish. Top each pancake with a little butter and drizzle with maple syrup. Serve with grilled bacon.

Energy 46Kcal/196kJ; Protein 1.8g; Carbohydrate 7.9g, of which sugars 1.3g; Fat 1.1g, of which saturates 0.3g; Cholesterol 23mg; Calcium 25mg; Fibre 0.3g; Sodium 12mg.

IRISH GRIDDLE SCONES

ALSO CALLED POTATO CAKES OR GRIDDLE CAKES, THESE DELICIOUS MORSELS ARE GREAT WITH BUTTER AND JAM, OR WITH BACON FOR A HEARTY MORNING-AFTER BREAKFAST OR BRUNCH.

MAKES SIX

INGREDIENTS

225g/8oz floury potatoes, cut into
   uniform chunks
115g/4oz/1 cup plain (all-purpose)
   flour
2.5ml/½ tsp salt
2.5ml/½ tsp baking powder
50g/2oz/4 tbsp butter, diced
25ml/1½ tbsp milk
bacon rashers (strips), to serve
butter, for greasing

1 Cook the potatoes in a pan of boiling water until tender.

4 Add the mashed potatoes and mix thoroughly with a fork. Make a well in the centre and pour in the milk. Mix to form a smooth dough.

5 Turn out on to a lightly floured surface and knead gently for about 5 minutes until soft and pliable. Roll out to a round 5mm/¼ in thick. Cut in half, then cut each half into three wedges.

6 Before you cook the scones, fry a batch of bacon rashers to serve with them. Keep warm in a low oven, until the scones are ready.

7 Grease a griddle or frying pan with a little butter and heat until very hot. Add the cakes and fry for 3–4 minutes until golden brown on both sides turning once. Serve hot with the bacon rashers.

2 Drain the potatoes and return them to the pan over a high heat. Using a wooden spoon, stir the potatoes for 1 minute until moisture has evaporated. Transfer to a bowl and mash well, making sure there are no lumps.

3 Sift together the flour, salt and baking powder into a bowl. Rub in the butter with your fingertips until it has the consistency of fine breadcrumbs.

Energy 156Kcal/653kJ; Protein 2.6g; Carbohydrate 21.2g, of which sugars 1g; Fat 7.3g, of which saturates 4.5g; Cholesterol 18mg; Calcium 36mg; Fibre 1g; Sodium 221mg.

SCRAMBLED EGGS WITH ANCHOVIES

SCRAMBLED EGGS ARE WEANING FOOD AND THEY RATE HIGH IN THE COMFORT ZONE. JUST PLAIN ON LOTS OF BUTTERY TOAST, THEY WORK WONDERS FOR LIFTING THE SPIRITS.

SERVES TWO

INGREDIENTS
    2 slices bread
    40g/1½oz/3 tbsp butter, plus
       extra for spreading
    anchovy paste, such as
       Gentleman's Relish, for spreading
    2 eggs and 2 egg yolks, beaten
    60–90ml/4–6 tbsp single (light)
       cream or milk
    salt and ground black pepper
    anchovy fillets, cut into strips,
       and paprika, to garnish

COOK'S TIP
These creamy scrambled eggs are delicious in baked potatoes instead of on toast. Serve with a salad and a glass of crisp white wine for a tasty lunch.

1 Toast the bread, spread with butter and anchovy paste, then remove the crusts and cut into triangles. Keep warm.

2 Melt the rest of the butter in a medium non-stick pan, then stir in the beaten eggs, cream or milk, and a little salt and pepper. Heat very gently, stirring constantly, until the mixture begins to thicken.

3 Remove the pan from the heat and continue to stir until the mixture becomes very creamy, but do not allow it to harden.

4 Divide the scrambled eggs among the triangles of toast and garnish each one with strips of anchovy fillet and a generous sprinkling of paprika. Serve immediately, while still hot.

Energy 410Kcal/1701kJ; Protein 13.8g; Carbohydrate 11.3g, of which sugars 1.3g; Fat 35g, of which saturates 17.5g; Cholesterol 489mg; Calcium 104mg; Fibre 1.5g; Sodium 358mg.

OMELETTE ARNOLD BENNETT

CREATED FOR THE WRITER ARNOLD BENNETT, WHO DINED AT THE SAVOY HOTEL IN LONDON, THIS CREAMY, SMOKED HADDOCK SOUFFLÉ OMELETTE IS A FAVOURITE BREAKFAST TREAT.

SERVES TWO

INGREDIENTS

175g/6oz smoked haddock fillet, poached and drained
50g/2oz/4 tbsp butter, diced
175ml/6fl oz/¾ cup whipping or double (heavy) cream
4 eggs, separated
40g/1½oz/⅓ cup mature Cheddar cheese, grated
ground black pepper
watercress, to garnish

COOK'S TIP
In a comfort food emergency, when smoked haddock may not be available, use drained and flaked canned tuna or salmon instead.

1 Remove the skin and any bones from the haddock fillet and discard. Carefully flake the flesh using a fork.

2 Melt half the butter with 60ml/4 tbsp of the cream in a fairly small non-stick pan, then add the flaked fish and stir together gently. Cover the pan with a lid, remove from the heat and set aside to cool slightly.

3 Mix the egg yolks with 15ml/1 tbsp of the cream. Season with pepper, then stir into the fish. In a separate bowl, mix the cheese and the remaining cream. Stiffly whisk the egg whites, then fold into the fish mixture. Heat the remaining butter in an omelette pan, add the fish mixture and cook until browned underneath. Pour the cheese mixture over and grill (broil) until bubbling. Garnish and serve.

Energy 850Kcal/3518kJ; Protein 38.6g; Carbohydrate 2.6g, of which sugars 2.6g; Fat 76.2g, of which saturates 43.3g; Cholesterol 653mg; Calcium 291mg; Fibre 0g; Sodium 1151mg.

MUFFINS WITH BACON AND EGGS

THIS TASTY DISH IS IDEAL FOR BIRTHDAYS WHEN YOU WANT TO TREAT SOMEONE SPECIAL.

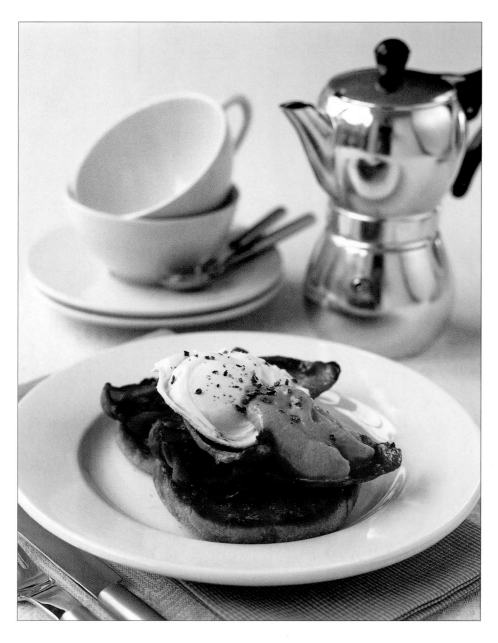

2 Fill a large frying pan with water and bring to the boil. Add the vinegar and regulate the heat so that the water simmers. Crack the eggs into the water and poach them for 3–4 minutes, or slightly longer for firm eggs.

3 Split and toast the muffins while the eggs are cooking. Spread with butter and place on warmed plates.

4 To make the hollandaise sauce, process the egg yolks and white wine vinegar in a blender or food processor. Melt the butter. With the motor still running, very gradually add the hot melted butter through the feeder tube. The hot butter will cook the yolks to make a thick, glossy sauce. Switch off the machine as soon as all the butter has been added and the sauce has thickened. Season to taste.

5 Arrange the bacon on the muffins and add a poached egg to each. Top with a spoonful of sauce and grind over some black pepper. Serve immediately.

SERVES FOUR

INGREDIENTS
   350g/12oz rindless back (lean)
    bacon rashers (strips)
   dash of white wine vinegar
   4 eggs
   4 English muffins
   butter, for spreading
   salt and ground black pepper
For the hollandaise sauce
   2 egg yolks
   5ml/1 tsp white wine vinegar
   75g/3oz/6 tbsp butter

1 Preheat the grill (broiler) and cook the bacon for 5–8 minutes, turning once, or until crisp on both sides.

COOK'S TIPS
• Eggs that are a week or more old will not keep their shape when poached so, for the best results, use very fresh free-range organic eggs.
• To make sure that you don't break the yolk, crack the eggs into a cup before carefully adding them to the gently simmering water.

Energy 612Kcal/2549kJ; Protein 32.6g; Carbohydrate 30.2g, of which sugars 2.4g; Fat 41.1g, of which saturates 18.3g; Cholesterol 429mg; Calcium 143mg; Fibre 1.3g; Sodium 1880mg.

FRIED POTATOES WITH CHORIZO AND EGG

THIS SUMPTUOUS SPANISH BREAKFAST WILL SET YOU UP FOR A DAY OF HARD PHYSICAL WORK IN THE GARDEN.

SERVES FOUR

INGREDIENTS

6 fresh jalapeño chillies
60ml/4 tbsp vegetable oil
1 onion, finely chopped
450g/1lb waxy potatoes, scrubbed
  and cut in 1cm/½in cubes
few sprigs of fresh oregano, chopped,
  plus extra, to garnish
75g/3oz/1 cup freshly grated
  Parmesan cheese (optional)
225g/8oz chorizo sausage, sliced
4 eggs

1 Dry roast the jalapeños in a griddle pan, turning them frequently so that the skins blacken but do not burn. Place them in a strong plastic bag and tie the top to keep the steam in. Set aside for 20 minutes.

2 Remove the jalapeños from the bag, peel off the skins and remove any stems. Cut them in half, scrape out the seeds, then chop the flesh finely.

3 Meanwhile, heat half the oil in a large heavy frying pan which has a lid. Add the onion and fry, stirring occasionally, for 3–4 minutes, until translucent, then add the potato cubes.

4 Stir to coat the potato cubes in oil, then cover the pan and cook over a moderate heat for 20–25 minutes, until the potatoes are tender. Shake the pan occasionally to stop them from sticking to the bottom.

5 When the potatoes are tender, push them to the side of the frying pan, then add the remaining oil.

6 When the oil is hot, spread out the potatoes and add the jalapeños. Cook over a high heat for 5–10 minutes, stirring carefully so that the potatoes turn golden but do not break up.

7 Add the oregano and Parmesan, if using. Mix gently, spoon on to a heated serving dish or plates and keep hot.

8 Fry the chorizo in any oil remaining in the pan until cooked and browned. Add to the potatoes. Fry the eggs to taste using the chorizo fat or fresh oil, as preferred. Add to the potatoes and serve at once, sprinkled with oregano.

Energy 186Kcal/776kJ; Protein 2.2g; Carbohydrate 19.9g, of which sugars 2.7g; Fat 11.4g, of which saturates 1.4g; Cholesterol 0mg; Calcium 13mg; Fibre 1.5g; Sodium 13mg.

EGGS RANCHEROS

THERE ARE MANY VARIATIONS ON THIS POPULAR DISH, WHICH IS GREAT FOR BREAKFAST OR BRUNCH.
THE COMBINATION OF CREAMY EGGS WITH ONION, CHILLI AND TOMATOES WORKS WONDERFULLY WELL.

SERVES FOUR

INGREDIENTS

   oil, for frying
   2 corn tortillas, several days old, cut
     into strips
   2 fresh green jalapeño chillies
   1 garlic clove
   4 spring onions (scallions)
   1 large tomato
   8 eggs, beaten
   150ml/¼ pint/⅔ cup single (light)
     cream
   chopped fresh coriander (cilantro)
   salt and ground black pepper

1 Heat 1cm/½in oil in a frying pan until very hot, watching it closely. Fry the tortilla strips until golden, turning occasionally; drain on kitchen paper.

2 Spear the chillies on a long-handled metal skewer and roast them over the flame of a gas burner until the skins blister and darken. Do not let the flesh burn. Alternatively, dry fry them in a griddle pan until the skins are scorched. Place them in a strong plastic bag and tie the top to keep the steam in. Set aside for 20 minutes.

3 Meanwhile, crush the garlic and chop the spring onions finely. Cut a cross in the base of the tomato. Place it in a heatproof bowl and pour over boiling water to cover. After 3 minutes lift the tomato out using a slotted spoon and plunge it into a bowl of cold water. Leave for a few minutes to cool.

4 Drain the tomato, remove the skin and cut it into four pieces. Using a teaspoon scoop out the seeds and the core, then dice the flesh finely.

5 Remove the chillies from the bag and peel off the skins. Cut off the stalks, then slit the chillies and scrape out the seeds. Chop the flesh finely. Put the eggs in a bowl, season with salt and pepper and beat lightly.

6 Heat 15ml/1 tbsp oil in a large frying pan. Add the garlic and spring onions and fry gently for 2–3 minutes until soft. Stir in the diced tomato and cook for 3–4 minutes more, then stir in the chillies and cook for 1 minute.

7 Pour the eggs into the pan and stir until they start to set. When only a small amount of uncooked egg remains visible, stir in the cream so that the cooking process is slowed down and the mixture cooks to a creamy mixture rather than a solid mass.

8 Stir the chopped coriander into the scrambled egg. Arrange the tortilla strips on four serving plates and spoon the eggs over. Serve at once.

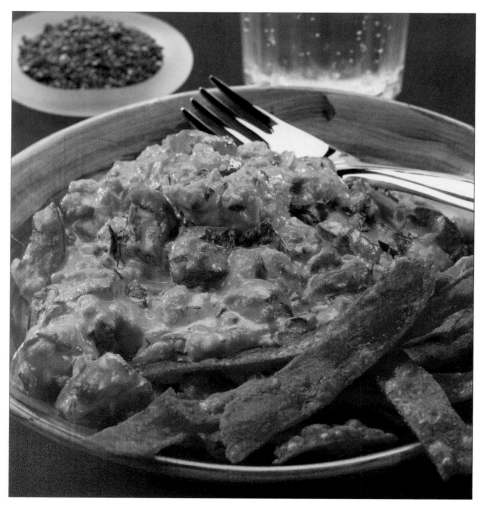

Energy 324Kcal/1355kJ; Protein 18.4g; Carbohydrate 17.8g, of which sugars 3.1g; Fat 20.9g, of which saturates 8.3g; Cholesterol 477mg; Calcium 146mg; Fibre 1.2g; Sodium 254mg.

BLACK PUDDING SNACKETTES

THIS IS A TRENDY TAKE ON THAT BREAKFAST FAVOURITE, FRIED BLACK PUDDING. MAKE IT WITH BLACK PUDDING OR MORCILLA — THE SPANISH BLACK PUDDING SEASONED WITH GARLIC AND OREGANO. THESE SNACKETTES ARE POPPED AWAY ONE AFTER THE OTHER, SO BE SURE TO MAKE PLENTY.

SERVES FOUR

INGREDIENTS
 15ml/1 tbsp olive oil
 1 onion, thinly sliced
 2 garlic cloves, thinly sliced
 5ml/1 tsp dried oregano
 5ml/1 tsp paprika
 225g/8oz black pudding (blood
  sausage), cut into 12 thick slices
 1 thin French stick, sliced into 12
 30ml/2 tbsp fino sherry
 sugar, to taste
 salt and ground black pepper
 chopped fresh oregano, to garnish

COOK'S TIP
If you can find real *morcilla*, serve it neat: simply fry the slices in olive oil and use to top little rounds of bread. If you cannot find black pudding, you can use red chorizo instead.

1 Heat the olive oil in a large frying pan and fry the sliced onion, garlic, oregano and paprika for 7–8 minutes until the onion is softened and has turned golden brown.

2 Add the slices of black pudding, then increase the heat and cook them for 3 minutes, without stirring. Turn them over carefully with a spatula and cook for a further 3 minutes until crisp.

3 Arrange the rounds of bread on a large serving plate and top each with a slice of black pudding. Stir the sherry into the onions and add a little sugar to taste. Heat, swirling the mixture around the pan until bubbling, then season with salt and black pepper.

4 Spoon a little of the onion mixture on top of each slice of black pudding. Scatter the oregano over and serve.

Energy 513Kcal/2164kJ; Protein 16.2g; Carbohydrate 77.4g, of which sugars 4.8g; Fat 16.7g, of which saturates 5.1g; Cholesterol 24mg; Calcium 213mg; Fibre 3.2g; Sodium 1208mg.

CHEER-ME-UPS

*The very thought of preparing some dishes is
enlivening. This chapter is full of foods that are
just right for times when other things are going
wrong. Tempting sandwiches and toddler suppers
are included along with grown-up recipes that
bring back memories of happy times. From boiled
eggs with toast fingers to sticky buns, there's a
recipe to cheer up every mood.*

JAMMY TOAST

THE SIMPLEST SNACKS WITH MINIMAL INGREDIENTS ARE OFTEN THE TREATS THAT TASTE THE BEST.
FLAVOURING THE BUTTER IS NOT ESSENTIAL BUT MAKES A NICE TOUCH.

SERVES TWO

INGREDIENTS
    75g/3oz/6 tbsp butter
    a little natural vanilla extract
    grated rind of 1 lemon (optional)
    4 slices bread
    20ml/4 tsp jam (jelly)

1 Cream the butter with vanilla to taste until thoroughly combined. Mix in the lemon rind, if using.

2 Toast the bread on both sides. Serve piping hot or leave to cool on a rack until crisp if preferred. Spread thickly with flavoured butter and jam, and eat at once.

Energy 445Kcal/1854kJ; Protein 4.4g; Carbohydrate 38.1g, of which sugars 13.1g; Fat 31.7g, of which saturates 19.8g; Cholesterol 80mg; Calcium 90mg; Fibre 1.7g; Sodium 475mg.

SMOKED MACKEREL PÂTÉ

SOME OF THE MOST DELICIOUS DISHES ARE ALSO THE EASIEST TO MAKE. SERVE THIS POPULAR PÂTÉ
WITH THIN MELBA OR HOT WHOLEMEAL (WHOLE-WHEAT) TOAST FOR A DEEPLY SATISFYING SNACK.

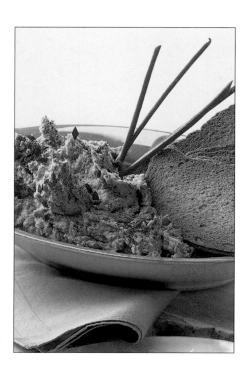

SERVES SIX

INGREDIENTS
    4 smoked mackerel fillets, skinned
    225g/8oz/1 cup cream cheese
    1–2 garlic cloves, finely chopped
    juice of 1 lemon
    30ml/2 tbsp chopped fresh chervil,
      parsley or chives
    15ml/1 tbsp Worcestershire sauce
    salt and cayenne pepper
    chopped fresh chives, to garnish

1 Break up the mackerel, discarding the skin and bones, and place in a food processor. Add the cream cheese, garlic, lemon juice and chervil, parsley or chives.

2 Process the ingredients until combined but with a slightly coarse texture, not completely smooth.

3 Add the Worcestershire sauce, salt and cayenne pepper to taste. Process to mix, then spoon the pâté into a dish, cover with clear film (plastic wrap) and chill for at least 30 minutes.

4 Sprinkle with chopped chives to garnish and serve.

Energy 402Kcal/1661kJ; Protein 13.8g; Carbohydrate 0.4g, of which sugars 0.4g; Fat 38.4g, of which saturates 15.3g; Cholesterol 106mg; Calcium 55mg; Fibre 0g; Sodium 643mg.

GARLIC MUSHROOMS <u>ON</u> TOAST

PUNCHY FLAVOUR AND RICH BUTTERY JUICES TASTE DIVINE IN THIS SIMPLE SUPPER TREAT.

SERVES FOUR

INGREDIENTS
  4 large slices bread
  75g/3oz/6 tbsp butter, plus extra
    melted butter for brushing bread
  3 shallots, finely chopped
  2 garlic cloves, finely chopped
  675g/1½lb field (portabello) or
    chestnut mushrooms, thickly sliced
  75ml/5 tbsp dry white wine
  45ml/3 tbsp chopped fresh parsley
  salt and ground black pepper

1 Toast the bread on both sides under a hot grill (broiler). Alternatively, heat a ridged griddle until very hot and toast the bread on both sides until quite dark. Brush the toasted bread with melted butter and keep warm.

2 Melt the butter in a frying pan, add the shallots and garlic, and cook for 5 minutes until golden. Add the mushrooms and toss well. Fry over a high heat for 1 minute.

3 Pour in the wine and season well. Boil over high heat until the wine evaporates and the mushrooms are moist and buttery. Lightly stir in the parsley. Pile the mushrooms on the toast and serve immediately.

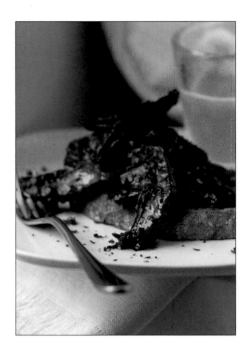

Energy 297Kcal/1240kJ; Protein 8.1g; Carbohydrate 25.9g, of which sugars 2.9g; Fat 17.3g, of which saturates 10.2g; Cholesterol 40mg; Calcium 107mg; Fibre 3.3g; Sodium 420mg.

CINNAMON TOAST

THIS IS AN OLD-FASHIONED SNACK THAT IS WARMING AND SOOTHING ON A COLD DAY. CINNAMON TOAST IS PERFECT WITH A HOT CHOCOLATE DRINK OR WITH FRESH FRUIT.

SERVES TWO

INGREDIENTS
  75g/3oz/6 tbsp butter
  2 teaspoons ground cinnamon
  30ml/2 tbsp caster (superfine) sugar
  4 slices bread
  prepared fresh fruit (optional)

1 Cream the butter with the cinnamon and half the sugar.

2 Toast the bread on both sides. Spread with the butter and sprinkle with a little extra sugar. Serve at once, with pieces of fresh fruit, if you like.

Energy 451Kcal/1877kJ; Protein 4.4g; Carbohydrate 39.6g, of which sugars 14.6g; Fat 31.7g, of which saturates 19.8g; Cholesterol 80mg; Calcium 94mg; Fibre 1.7g; Sodium 471mg.

CROQUE MONSIEUR

A POPULAR FRENCH SNACK THAT LITERALLY TRANSLATED MEANS "CRUNCH (OR MUNCH) GENTLEMAN".
TRADITIONALLY FRIED, BUT OFTEN TOASTED, THIS IS IDEAL WHEN INSTANT COMFORT IS REQUIRED.

SERVES TWO

INGREDIENTS
 a little butter, for spreading
 4 thin slices of country-style bread
 75g/3oz Gruyère or Cheddar
   cheese, sliced
 2 lean honey roast ham slices
 ground black pepper
 flat leaf parsley, to garnish

1 Preheat a sandwich toaster or the grill (broiler). Lightly butter the bread and place the cheese and ham on 2 slices. Top with the other slices of bread and press firmly together.

2 Cook in the sandwich toaster or under the grill until browned on both sides. Serve hot, garnished with parsley.

Energy 480Kcal/2010kJ; Protein 20.9g; Carbohydrate 48.6g, of which sugars 3.1g; Fat 22.9g, of which saturates 14g; Cholesterol 65mg; Calcium 452mg; Fibre 2.1g; Sodium 1072mg.

WELSH RAREBIT

THIS HAS BEEN A FAVOURITE SNACK FOR GENERATIONS. TRADITIONALLY, THE CHEESE IS MELTED WITH
BUTTER, A LITTLE BEER, MUSTARD AND SEASONING, THEN SPREAD ON TOAST, BUT THIS IS A QUICK AND
QUIRKY VERSION. USE GOOD MELTING CHEESE, SUCH AS CHEDDAR, MONTEREY JACK OR CAERPHILLY.

SERVES TWO

INGREDIENTS
 2 thick slices bread
 butter, for spreading
 10ml/2 tsp spicy or mild mustard
 100g/3¾oz Cheddar cheese, sliced
 pinch of paprika or cayenne pepper
 ground black pepper

1 Preheat the grill (broiler) and lightly toast the bread on both sides. Spread with butter and mustard, then top with the cheese. Heat under the grill until the cheese melts and starts to brown.

2 Sprinkle a little paprika or cayenne on the cheese. Season with pepper.

Energy 363Kcal/1516kJ; Protein 17.3g; Carbohydrate 24.3g, of which sugars 1.6g; Fat 21.5g, of which saturates 13.7g; Cholesterol 59mg; Calcium 457mg; Fibre 1.1g; Sodium 687mg.

BOILED EGG WITH TOAST SOLDIERS

IT IS A GOOD IDEA TO GET BACK TO BASICS OCCASIONALLY AND THIS IS ONE OF THE FIRST EATING EXPERIENCES MOST PEOPLE HAVE. EGGS AND TOAST ARE NUTRITIOUS, WARMING AND COMFORTING. TOAST SOLDIERS HAVE A SMILE-A-DIP QUALITY THAT IS JUST UNBEATABLE.

SERVES ONE

INGREDIENTS
 1 egg
 4 thin slices bread
 a little butter, for spreading
 salt

1 Place the egg in a small pan and pour in hot, not boiling, water to cover. Bring to the boil and cook for 3 minutes for a very soft egg, 4 minutes for a soft yolk and firm white, or 8 minutes for a hard egg.

2 Toast the bread while the egg is boiling and cut it into fingers. Serve the freshly boiled egg with toast fingers, butter and salt to sprinkle.

Energy 409Kcal/1710kJ; Protein 12.5g; Carbohydrate 40.3g, of which sugars 2.8g; Fat 23.1g, of which saturates 12.3g; Cholesterol 235mg; Calcium 154mg; Fibre 2.5g; Sodium 556mg.

POACHED EGG ON TOAST

BUY THE FRESHEST EGGS AS THEIR WHITES ARE NOT TOO RUNNY, SO THEY STAY IN SHAPE DURING COOKING. ADD A LITTLE VINEGAR TO THE SIMMERING WATER TO HELP THE WHITE SET QUICKLY AND SWIRL THE WATER BEFORE DROPPING IN THE EGG. A COMFORTING SUPPER IN JUST A FEW MINUTES.

SERVES ONE

INGREDIENTS
 1 red or green (bell) pepper or a
  mixture of both
 1 spring onion (scallion), chopped
 75g/3oz/6 tbsp butter
 chilli flakes (optional)
 2 eggs
 2 thin slices toast
 salt and ground black pepper

1 Cook the pepper and spring onions in the butter until soft. Add chilli if liked.

2 Poach the eggs in a frying pan of simmering water for 3–4 minutes, until set. Arrange the peppers and eggs on toast and serve at once.

Energy 891Kcal/3692kJ; Protein 19.4g; Carbohydrate 39.4g, of which sugars 13.2g; Fat 74.3g, of which saturates 42.5g; Cholesterol 540mg; Calcium 146mg; Fibre 3.8g; Sodium 914mg.

CLASSIC EGG MAYO SANDWICH

WHEN THE EGG IS PERFECTLY HARD-BOILED, THE MAYONNAISE FRESHLY MADE AND THE BREAD SOFT AND CRUSTY, THIS IS ONE OF THE MOST SATISFYING SANDWICHES TO EAT.

SERVES TWO

INGREDIENTS
    4 eggs
    4 spring onions (scallions), chopped
    1 dill-pickled cucumber, chopped
    softened butter
    4 thick slices bread
    mustard and cress, watercress, or
      rocket (arugula)
    salt and ground black pepper
For the mayonnaise
    2 egg yolks
    2.5ml/½ tsp Dijon or English (hot)
      mustard
    300ml/½ pint/1¼ cups mild olive oil
    15ml/1 tbsp white wine vinegar or a
      squeeze of lemon juice
    salt and ground black pepper

1 Make the mayonnaise. Beat the egg yolks with the mustard and salt in a bowl. Add half the oil a tablespoon at a time and whisk in each addition until the mixture begins to thicken. Add the vinegar or lemon juice and beat again. Add the remaining oil in a thin, steady stream, beating all the time. Season. Chill.

2 Place the eggs in a pan and cover with cold water. Simmer for 7 minutes. Drain and immerse in cold water.

3 Peel and roughly chop the eggs. Add the spring onions, cucumber and enough mayonnaise to make a thick, spreadable mixture.

4 Butter the bread. Sprinkle with cress, watercress or rocket and pile the filling on top. Top with bread.

Energy 680Kcal/2819kJ; Protein 15g; Carbohydrate 30.2g, of which sugars 3.5g; Fat 56.5g, of which saturates 13.6g; Cholesterol 35mg; Calcium 201mg; Fibre 2.3g; Sodium 479mg.

CHICKEN TIKKA SANDWICH

USING COOKED CHICKEN TIKKA TO FILL A SANDWICH IS A GREAT WAY OF ENJOYING THE SPICINESS OF INDIAN FOOD WITHOUT HAVING TO PREPARE OR BUY A WHOLE MEAL.

SERVES ONE

INGREDIENTS
    1 chicken tikka breast
    butter for spreading
    2 thick slices wholemeal (whole-
      wheat) bread
    mango chutney
    watercress sprigs

1 Slice the chicken tikka thinly. Butter the bread and spread one slice with a little mango chutney.

2 Arrange the chicken on the bread and top with watercress sprigs. Cover with the second slice of bread and press down gently.

Nutritional information per portion: Energy 360Kcal/1525kJ; Protein 35.9g; Carbohydrate 43.3g, of which sugars 16.5g; Fat 6g, of which saturates 0.7g; Cholesterol 88mg; Calcium 139mg; Fibre 2.3g; Sodium 729mg.

CHEESE SALAD BAGUETTE

ONE OF THE MOST POPULAR OF ALL SANDWICHES. CHEESE IS A STAPLE PART OF MANY PEOPLE'S DIETS AND ITS FAMILIARITY MAKES IT TRULY COMFORTING. ADD YOUR CHOICE OF SALAD AND PICKLE.

SERVES ONE

INGREDIENTS
  1 small baguette
  butter for spreading
  3 slices hard cheese, such as
    Cheddar, Red Leicester, Spanish
    Manchego or Monterey Jack
  2 tomatoes, sliced
  ½ small red or white onion
  watercress sprigs
  mixed salad leaves
  salt and pepper

1 Slit the baguette open lengthways and spread with butter. Insert the cheese, cutting large slices in half so that they fit.

2 Add the tomatoes and the onion, separating the slices into rings. Season lightly with salt and pepper.

3 Insert some watercress and salad leaves and press the baguette closed.

Nutritional information per portion: Energy 700Kcal/2931kJ; Protein 25.8g; Carbohydrate 64.1g, of which sugars 9.4g; Fat 38.4g, of which saturates 23.9g; Cholesterol 101mg; Calcium 590mg; Fibre 4.2g; Sodium 1182mg.

CLASSIC BLT

THIS DELICIOUS AMERICAN SANDWICH IS MADE WITH CRISPY BACON, LETTUCE AND TOMATO. CHOOSE THE BREAD YOU PREFER AND TOAST IT IF YOU LIKE.

MAKES TWO

INGREDIENTS
  4 slices Granary (whole-wheat) bread
  15g/½oz/1 tbsp softened butter
  few crisp cos, romaine or iceberg
    lettuce leaves
  1 large tomato, sliced
  8 rashers (strips) streaky (fatty)
    bacon
  30ml/2 tbsp mayonnaise

1 Spread two of the slices of bread with butter. Lay the lettuce over the bread and cover with sliced tomato.

2 Grill (broil) the bacon rashers until they begin to crisp, then arrange them over the sliced tomato.

3 Quickly spread the two remaining slices of bread with mayonnaise. Lay the bread over the bacon, press the sandwiches together gently and cut in half. Serve immediately.

Energy 587Kcal/2439kJ; Protein 17.5g; Carbohydrate 28.2g, of which sugars 3g; Fat 46.1g, of which saturates 8.5g; Cholesterol 414mg; Calcium 150mg; Fibre 2g; Sodium 587mg.

FRIED MOZZARELLA SANDWICH

THIS IS REASSURING SNACKING ITALIAN STYLE, WITH GLORIOUS MELTING MOZZARELLA IN CRISP FRIED EGG-SOAKED BREAD. THE RESULT IS A DELICIOUS SAVOURY SANDWICH.

MAKES TWO

INGREDIENTS
    115g/4oz mozzarella cheese,
      thickly sliced
    4 thick slices white bread
    1 egg
    30ml/2 tbsp milk
    vegetable oil, for frying
    salt and freshly ground black pepper
    tomato, to garnish

1 Place the cheese on two slices of bread and season to taste. Top with the remaining bread to make two cheese sandwiches.

2 Beat the egg with the milk. Season with salt and pepper to taste and pour into a shallow dish.

3 Carefully dip the sandwiches into the egg and milk mixture until thoroughly coated. Leave to soak while heating the oil in a large, heavy frying pan.

4 Fry the sandwiches, in batches if necessary, until golden brown and crisp on both sides. Remove from the frying pan and drain well on kitchen paper. Garnish with tomato.

VARIATION
Use any favourite cheese instead of mozzarella. Add some chopped spring onions (scallions) and sliced cooked ham or salami before sandwiching the bread together.

Energy 429Kcal/1789kJ; Protein 18.9g; Carbohydrate 30.5g, of which sugars 2.7g; Fat 26.6g, of which saturates 10.4g; Cholesterol 129mg; Calcium 331mg; Fibre 1.9g; Sodium 539mg.

TUNA MELT

THE COMBINATION OF TUNA AND GRILLED CHEESE OOZING OUT OF THE TOASTED BREAD MAKES THIS TOASTIE A HEAVENLY TREAT.

MAKES TWO

INGREDIENTS
    90g/3½oz can tuna, drained and
      flaked
    30ml/2 tbsp mayonnaise
    15ml/1 tbsp finely chopped celery
    15ml/1 tbsp finely chopped
      spring onion (scallion)
    15ml/1 tbsp chopped fresh parsley
    5ml/1 tsp lemon juice
    25g/1oz/2 tbsp softened butter
    4 slices wholemeal (whole-wheat)
      bread
    50g/2oz Gruyère or Emmenthal
      cheese, sliced
    salad leaves, tomatoes and corn,
      to garnish

1 Mix together the tuna, mayonnaise, celery, spring onion, parsley and lemon juice in a small bowl.

2 Butter the bread with half the butter and spread the tuna filling over two slices. Cover with the cheese, then sandwich with the remaining bread.

3 Butter the top of the bread and place under a medium grill (broiler) for 1–2 minutes. Turn over, spread with butter and grill (broil) for a further 1–2 minutes until the cheese begins to melt. Garnish with salad leaves, tomatoes and corn.

Energy 567Kcal/2356kJ; Protein 22.3g; Carbohydrate 23.3g, of which sugars 1.6g; Fat 42.8g, of which saturates 15.5g; Cholesterol 96mg; Calcium 231mg; Fibre 3.2g; Sodium 832mg.

STEAK CIABATTA <u>WITH</u> HUMMUS <u>AND</u> SALAD

PACKED WITH GARLICKY HUMMUS AND A MUSTARD-SEASONED DRESSING ON THE CRUNCHY SALAD,
THESE STEAK SANDWICHES HAVE A FILLING TO BE RECKONED WITH.

SERVES FOUR

INGREDIENTS
  3 garlic cloves, crushed to a paste
    with enough salt to season the
    steaks
  30ml/2 tbsp extra virgin olive oil
  4 sirloin steaks, 2.5cm/1in thick,
    total weight about 900g/2lb
  2 romaine lettuce hearts
  4 small ciabatta breads
  salt and ground black pepper
For the dressing
  10ml/2 tsp Dijon mustard
  5ml/1 tsp cider vinegar or white
    wine vinegar
  15ml/1 tbsp olive oil
For the hummus
  400g/14oz can chickpeas, drained
    and rinsed
  45ml/3 tbsp tahini
  2 garlic cloves, crushed
  juice of 1 lemon
  30ml/2 tbsp water

1 To make the hummus, place the
chickpeas in a food processor and
pulse to a paste. Add the tahini, garlic,
lemon juice, salt and pepper. Pour in
the water and pulse to mix.

2 Make a dressing by mixing the
mustard and vinegar in a jar. Add the oil
and season to taste. Shake well.

3 Mix the garlic and oil in a dish. Add
the steaks and rub the mixture into
both surfaces.

4 Preheat the grill (broiler). Cook the
steaks on a rack in a grill (broiling) pan.
For rare meat, allow 2 minutes on one
side and 3 minutes on the second side.
For medium steaks, allow 4 minutes on
each side. Transfer to a plate, cover and
rest for 2 minutes.

5 Dress the lettuce. Split each ciabatta
and heat on the grill rack for a minute.
Fill with hummus, the steaks and
leaves. Cut each in half to serve.

Energy 1060Kcal/4429kJ; Protein 75.9g; Carbohydrate 56.1g, of which sugars 3.5g; Fat 60.6g, of which saturates 11.6g; Cholesterol 115mg; Calcium 446mg; Fibre 9.6g; Sodium 791mg.

CORNISH PASTIES

These traditional pasties are made with a rich crumbly shortcrust that melts in the mouth. The filling is raw when enclosed in the pastry, so must be cooked thoroughly.

MAKES SIX

INGREDIENTS
   450g/1lb chuck steak, diced
   1 potato, about 175g/6oz, diced
   175g/6oz swede (rutabaga), diced
   1 onion, chopped
   2.5ml/½ tsp dried mixed herbs
   1 egg, beaten
   salt and ground black pepper
   salad, to garnish
For the pastry
   350g/12oz/3 cups plain
    (all-purpose) flour
   pinch of salt
   115g/4oz/½ cup butter, diced
   50g/2oz/¼ cup lard (shortening) or
    white vegetable fat
   75–90ml/5–6 tbsp chilled water

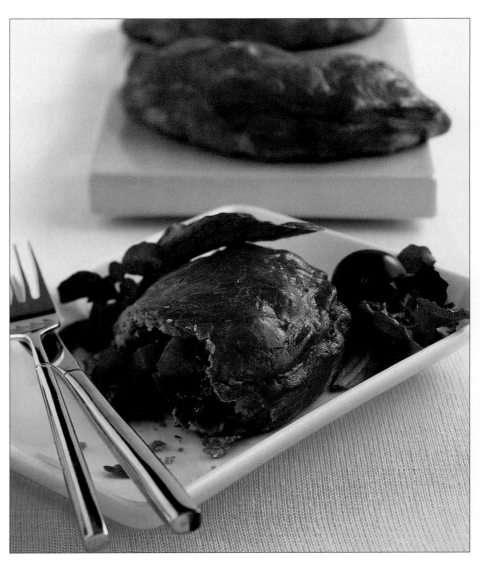

1 To make the pastry, sift the flour and salt into a bowl. Using your fingertips or a pastry blender, lightly rub or cut in the butter and lard or vegetable fat, then sprinkle over most of the chilled water and mix to a soft dough, adding more water if necessary. Knead the pastry on a lightly floured surface for a few seconds until smooth. Wrap in clear film (plastic wrap) and chill for 30 minutes.

2 Preheat the oven to 220°C/425°F/ Gas 7. Divide the pastry into six pieces, then roll out each piece on a lightly floured surface to a 20cm/8in round.

3 Mix together the steak, vegetables, herbs and seasoning in a bowl, then spoon an equal amount on to one half of each pastry round.

4 Brush the pastry edges with water, then fold the free half of each round over the filling. Press the edges firmly together to seal, then use your fingertips to crimp the edges.

5 Brush the pasties with the beaten egg. Bake for 15 minutes, then reduce the temperature to 160°C/325°F/Gas 3 and bake for 1 hour more. Serve the pasties hot or cold with a salad garnish.

Energy 554Kcal/2317kJ; Protein 22.9g; Carbohydrate 53g, of which sugars 3.4g; Fat 29.2g, of which saturates 15.3g; Cholesterol 96mg; Calcium 110mg; Fibre 2.9g; Sodium 238mg.

CURRIED LAMB SAMOSAS

FILO PASTRY IS PERFECT FOR MAKING SAMOSAS AND IS SO LIGHT YOU'LL BE ABLE TO EAT LOTS OF THEM! YOU'LL BE AMAZED AT HOW QUICK AND EASY THEY ARE TO MAKE.

MAKES TWELVE

INGREDIENTS
   25g/1oz/2 tbsp butter
   225g/8oz/1 cup minced (ground)
    lamb
   30ml/2 tbsp mild curry paste
   12 filo pastry sheets
   salt and ground black pepper

1 Heat a little butter in a large pan and add the lamb. Fry for 5–6 minutes, stirring occasionally until browned. Stir in the curry paste and cook for 1–2 minutes. Season and set aside. Preheat the oven to 190°/375°C/Gas 5.

2 Melt the remaining butter in a small pan. Cut the pastry sheets in half lengthways. Brush one strip of pastry lightly with butter, then lay another strip on top and brush lightly and evenly with more butter.

3 Place a spoonful of lamb in the corner of the strip and fold over to form a triangle at one end. Keep folding over in the same way to form a triangular package. Brush with butter and place on a baking sheet. Repeat using the remaining pastry. Bake for 15–20 minutes until golden. Serve hot.

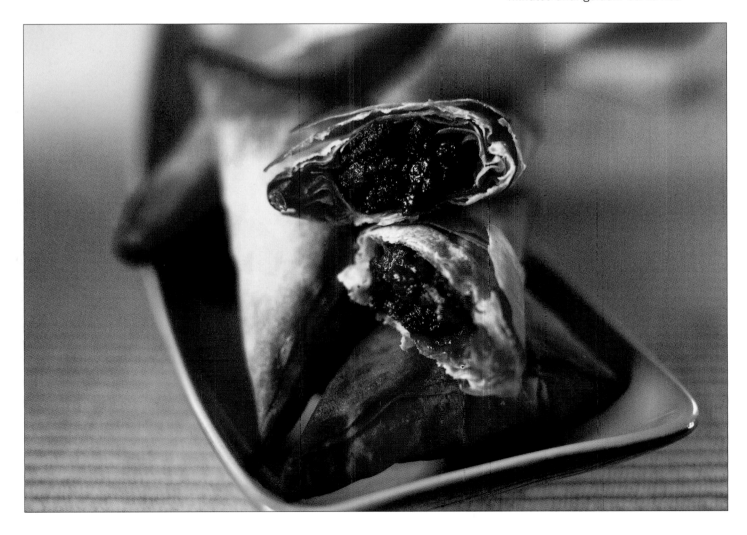

Energy 88Kcal/368kJ; Protein 4.6g; Carbohydrate 8.1g, of which sugars 0.2g; Fat 4.3g, of which saturates 2.3g; Cholesterol 19mg; Calcium 18mg; Fibre 0.3g; Sodium 26mg.

HUMMUS

THIS CLASSIC MIDDLE EASTERN DISH IS MADE FROM COOKED CHICKPEAS, GROUND TO A PASTE AND FLAVOURED WITH GARLIC, LEMON JUICE, TAHINI, OLIVE OIL AND CUMIN. IT IS DELICIOUS SERVED WITH WEDGES OF TOASTED PITTA BREAD OR CRUDITÉS.

SERVES FOUR TO SIX

INGREDIENTS
    400g/14oz can chickpeas, drained
    60ml/4 tbsp tahini
    2–3 garlic cloves, chopped
    juice of ½–1 lemon
    cayenne pepper
    small pinch to 1.5ml/¼ tsp ground
      cumin, to taste
    salt and ground black pepper

1 Using a potato masher or food processor coarsely mash the chickpeas. If you prefer a smoother purée, process them in a food processor or blender until smooth.

2 Mix the tahini into the chickpeas, then stir in the garlic, lemon juice, cayenne, cumin, and salt and pepper to taste. If needed, add a little water. Serve at room temperature.

Energy 461Kcal/1917kJ; Protein 17.8g; Carbohydrate 16.6g, of which sugars 0.6g; Fat 36.5g, of which saturates 5.1g; Cholesterol 0mg; Calcium 431mg; Fibre 8.7g; Sodium 232mg.

TARAMASALATA

THIS TASTY DIP MAKES AN EXCELLENT SNACK ON DULL DAYS, REVIVING MEMORIES OF HOLIDAYS IN THE SUN AND RELAXED EVENINGS SIPPING WELL-CHILLED WINE.

1 Place the smoked roe, garlic, onion, oil, bread and lemon juice in a blender or food processor and process until smooth. Add the milk or water and process again for a few seconds. (This will give the taramasalata a creamier texture.)

2 Pour the taramasalata into a bowl, cover with clear film (plastic wrap) and chill for 1–2 hours before serving. Sprinkle the dip with ground black pepper. Serve with warm pitta bread.

SERVES FOUR

INGREDIENTS
    115g/4oz smoked mullet roe
    2 garlic cloves, crushed
    30ml/2 tbsp grated onion
    60ml/4 tbsp olive oil
    4 slices white bread, crusts removed
    juice of 2 lemons
    30ml/2 tbsp milk or water
    freshly ground black pepper
    warm pitta bread, to serve

Energy 194Kcal/808kJ; Protein 8.6g; Carbohydrate 13.6g, of which sugars 1.6g; Fat 12.1g, of which saturates 1.7g; Cholesterol 95mg; Calcium 36mg; Fibre 0.6g; Sodium 1145mg.

POTATO SKINS WITH CAJUN DIP

DIVINELY CRISP AND NAUGHTY, THESE POTATO SKINS ARE GREAT ON THEIR OWN OR SERVED WITH THEIR PIQUANT DIP AS A DRIZZLED TOPPING OR ON THE SIDE.

SERVES TWO

INGREDIENTS
2 large baking potatoes
vegetable oil, for deep-frying
For the dip
120ml/4fl oz/½ cup natural (plain)
   yogurt
1 garlic clove, crushed
5ml/1 tsp tomato purée (paste)
2.5ml/½ tsp green chilli purée or
   ½ small green chilli, chopped
1.5ml/¼ tsp celery salt
salt and ground black pepper

COOK'S TIP
If you prefer, you can microwave the potatoes to save time. This will take about 10 minutes.

1 Preheat the oven to 180°C/350°F/ Gas 4. Bake the potatoes for 45–50 minutes until tender. Cut them in half and scoop out the flesh, leaving a thin layer on the skins.

2 To make the dip, mix together all the ingredients and chill.

3 Heat a 1cm/½in layer of oil in a large pan or deep fryer. Cut each potato half in half again, then fry them until crisp and golden on both sides. Drain on kitchen paper, sprinkle with salt and black pepper and serve with a bowl of dip or a dollop of dip in each skin.

Energy 265Kcal/1095kJ; Protein 3.8g; Carbohydrate 12.2g, of which sugars 5g; Fat 22.8g, of which saturates 2.9g; Cholesterol 1mg; Calcium 121mg; Fibre 0.8g; Sodium 350mg.

PAIN AU CHOCOLAT

A FRESHLY BAKED PAIN AU CHOCOLAT IS ALMOST IMPOSSIBLE TO RESIST, WITH ITS BUTTERY, FLAKY YET CRISP PASTRY CONCEALING A DELECTABLE CHOCOLATE FILLING. FOR A SPECIAL FINISH, DRIZZLE MELTED CHOCOLATE OVER THE TOPS OF THE FRESHLY BAKED PASTRIES.

MAKES NINE

INGREDIENTS
    250g/9oz/2¼ cups strong unbleached
      white bread flour
    30ml/2 tbsp skimmed milk powder
      (non fat dry milk)
    15ml/1 tbsp caster (superfine) sugar
    2.5ml/½ tsp salt
    7.5ml/1½ tsp easy-blend (rapid-rise)
      dried yeast
    140g/5oz/⅔ cup butter, softened
    125ml/4½fl oz/generous ½ cup hand-
      hot water
    225g/8oz plain (semisweet)
      chocolate, broken into pieces
For the glaze
    1 egg yolk
    15ml/1 tbsp milk

1 Mix the flour, milk powder, sugar and salt in a bowl. Stir in the yeast and make a well in the middle of these dry ingredients. Melt 25g/1oz/2 tbsp of the butter and add it to the dry ingredients, pouring it into the well in the middle of the mixture. Pour in the water and then mix to form a firm dough.

2 Turn the dough out on to a lightly floured surface and knead it thoroughly for about 10 minutes, until it is smooth and elastic. When pressed on the surface it should spring back rather than retain the dent.

3 Dust the bowl with flour and return the dough to it. Cover with clear film (plastic wrap) and leave in a warm place until doubled in size.

4 Meanwhile shape the remaining softened butter into an oblong block, about 2cm/¾in thick.

5 Lightly grease two baking sheets. When the dough has doubled in size, turn it out on to a floured surface. Knock back (punch down) and shape into a ball. Cut a cross halfway through the top of the dough.

6 Roll out around the cross, leaving a risen centre. Place the butter in the centre. Fold the rolled dough over the butter to enclose; seal the edges.

7 Roll to a rectangle 2cm/¾in thick, twice as long as wide. Fold the bottom third up and the top down; seal the edges with a rolling pin. Wrap in lightly oiled clear film. Place in the refrigerator and chill for 20 minutes.

8 Do the same again twice more, giving a quarter turn and chilling each time. Chill again for 30 minutes.

9 Roll out the dough to a rectangle measuring 52 x 30cm/21 x 12in. Using a sharp knife, cut the dough into three strips lengthways and widthways to make nine 18 x 10cm/7 x 4in rectangles.

10 Divide the chocolate among the three dough rectangles, placing the pieces lengthways at one short end.

11 Mix the egg yolk and milk for the glaze together. Brush the mixture over the edges of the dough.

12 Roll up each piece of dough to completely enclose the chocolate, then press the edges together to seal.

13 Place the pastries seam side down on the prepared baking sheets. Cover with oiled clear film and leave to rise in a warm place for about 30 minutes or until doubled in size.

14 Meanwhile, preheat the oven to 200°C/400°F/Gas 6. Brush the pastries with the remaining glaze and bake for about 15 minutes, or until golden. Turn out on to a wire rack to cool just slightly and serve warm.

VARIATION
Fill this flaky yeast pastry with a variety of sweet and savoury fillings. Try chopped nuts, tossed with a little brown sugar and cinnamon or, for a savoury filling, thin strips of cheese, wrapped in ham or mixed with chopped cooked bacon.

Energy 345Kcal/1441kJ; Protein 4g; Carbohydrate 39.3g, of which sugars 17.9g; Fat 20.1g, of which saturates 12.4g; Cholesterol 35mg; Calcium 51mg; Fibre 1.5g; Sodium 206mg.

CHELSEA BUNS

SAID TO HAVE BEEN INVENTED BY THE OWNER OF THE CHELSEA BUN HOUSE IN LONDON AT THE END OF THE 17TH CENTURY, CHELSEA BUNS MAKE THE PERFECT ACCOMPANIMENT TO A CUP OF COFFEE OR TEA. THEY ARE SO DELICIOUS, IT IS DIFFICULT TO RESIST EATING SEVERAL IN ONE SITTING!

MAKES TWELVE

INGREDIENTS
  500g/1lb 2oz/4½ cups strong
    unbleached white bread flour
  2.5ml/½ tsp salt
  50g/2oz/¼ cup butter, softened
  75g/3oz/6 tbsp caster (superfine)
    sugar
  5ml.1tsp easy-blend dried yeast
  225ml/8fl oz/scant 1 cup hand-hot
    milk
  1 egg, beaten
For the glaze
  50g/2oz/¼ cup caster (superfine)
    sugar
  5ml/1 tsp orange flower water
For the filling
  25g/1oz/2 tbsp butter, melted
  115g/4oz/⅔ cup sultanas
    (golden raisins)
  25g/1oz/3 tbsp mixed chopped
    (candied) peel
  25g/1oz/2 tbsp currants
  25g/1oz/2 tbsp soft light brown sugar
  5ml/1 tsp mixed (apple pie) spice

1 Mix the flour and salt in a large bowl, then rub in the butter and stir in the sugar and yeast.

2 Make a well in the middle of the dry ingredients and add the milk and egg. Mix the liquids into the dry ingredients to make a firm dough.

3 Turn the dough out on to a floured surface and knead thoroughly for about 10 minutes, until it is smooth and elastic. Flour the mixing bowl, return the dough to it and cover with oiled clear film (plastic wrap). Leave in a warm place until doubled in size.

4 Lightly grease a 23cm/9in square cake tin (pan). When the dough has risen, turn it out on to a floured surface and knock it back (punch it down).

5 Roll out the dough on a lightly floured surface into a square that measures about 30cm/12in.

6 Brush the dough with the melted butter for the filling and sprinkle it with the sultanas, mixed peel, currants, brown sugar and mixed spice, leaving a 1cm/½in border along one edge.

7 Starting at a covered edge, roll the dough up, Swiss (jelly) roll fashion. Press the edges together to seal. Cut the roll into 12 slices and then place these cut side uppermost in the prepared tin.

8 Cover with oiled clear film. Leave the buns to rise in a warm place for about 30–45 minutes, or until the dough slices have doubled in size and are almost at the top of the tin.

9 Meanwhile, preheat the oven to 200°C/400°F/Gas 6. Bake the buns for 15–20 minutes, or until they have risen well and are evenly golden all over.

10 Once they are baked, leave the buns to cool slightly in the tin before lifting them out and transferring them to a wire rack to cool.

11 Gently heat the ingredients for the glaze in a small pan until the sugar is dissolved. Brush the mixture over the warm buns. Serve slightly warm.

COOK'S TIP
Use icing (confectioners') sugar instead of caster sugar and make a thin glaze icing to brush or trickle over the freshly baked buns.

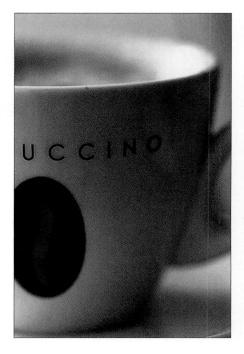

Energy 283Kcal/1199kJ; Protein 5g; Carbohydrate 55.7g, of which sugars 23.9g; Fat 6.1g, of which saturates 3.5g; Cholesterol 14mg; Calcium 99mg; Fibre 1.6g; Sodium 138mg.

COMFORTING
DISHES

*When you need something really tasty to eat,
the recipes in this chapter provide plenty of
options. Indisputably delicious, they are also
relatively simple to make without any need for
tricky techniques. Try a tasty Spanish Omelette
with a fresh green salad, or Hot Pepperoni Pizza
to share with friends.*

ROASTED ROOT VEGETABLE SOUP

ROASTING THE VEGETABLES GIVES THIS WINTER SOUP A WONDERFUL DEPTH OF FLAVOUR. YOU CAN USE OTHER VEGETABLES, IF YOU WISH, OR ADAPT THE QUANTITIES DEPENDING ON WHAT'S IN SEASON.

SERVES SIX

INGREDIENTS

50ml/2fl oz/¼ cup olive oil
1 small butternut squash, peeled, seeded and cubed
2 carrots, cut into thick rounds
1 large parsnip, cubed
1 small swede (rutabaga), cubed
2 leeks, thickly sliced
1 onion, quartered
3 bay leaves
4 thyme sprigs, plus extra to garnish
3 rosemary sprigs
1.2 litres/2 pints/5 cups vegetable stock
salt and freshly ground black pepper
sour cream, to serve

1 Preheat the oven to 200°C/400°F/ Gas 6. Put the olive oil into a large bowl. Add the prepared vegetables and toss until coated in the oil.

2 Spread out the vegetables in a single layer on one large or two small baking sheets. Tuck the herbs among the vegetables.

3 Roast for 50 minutes until tender, turning the vegetables occasionally to make sure they brown evenly. Remove from the oven, discard the herbs and transfer the vegetables to a large pan.

4 Pour the stock into the pan and bring to the boil. Reduce the heat, season to taste, then simmer for 10 minutes. Transfer the soup to a food processor or blender (or use a hand blender) and process for a few minutes until thick and smooth.

5 Return the soup to the pan to heat through. Season and serve with a swirl of sour cream. Garnish each serving with a sprig of thyme.

COOK'S TIP
Dried herbs can be used in place of fresh; sprinkle 2.5ml/½ tsp of each type over the vegetables in step 2.

Energy 134Kcal/563kJ; Protein 3g; Carbohydrate 17.2g, of which sugars 11.3g; Fat 6.5g, of which saturates 0.9g; Cholesterol 0mg; Calcium 96mg; Fibre 5.2g; Sodium 160mg.

ROASTED GARLIC AND BUTTERNUT SQUASH SOUP WITH TOMATO SALSA

THIS IS A WONDERFUL, RICHLY FLAVOURED DISH. A SPOONFUL OF THE HOT AND SPICY TOMATO SALSA GIVES BITE TO THE SWEET-TASTING SQUASH AND GARLIC SOUP.

SERVES FOUR TO FIVE

INGREDIENTS

2 garlic bulbs, outer papery
skin removed
75ml/5 tbsp olive oil
a few fresh thyme sprigs
1 large butternut squash, halved
and seeded
2 onions, chopped
5ml/1 tsp ground coriander
1.2 litres/2 pints/5 cups vegetable or
chicken stock
30–45ml/2–3 tbsp chopped fresh
oregano or marjoram
salt and ground black pepper
For the salsa
4 large ripe tomatoes, halved
and seeded
1 red (bell) pepper, halved and
seeded
1 large fresh red chilli, halved
and seeded
30–45ml/2–3 tbsp extra virgin
olive oil
15ml/1 tbsp balsamic vinegar
pinch of caster (superfine) sugar

1 Preheat the oven to 220°C/425°F/ Gas 7. Place the garlic on a piece of foil and pour over half the olive oil. Add the thyme sprigs, then fold the foil around the garlic bulbs to enclose them. Place the foil parcel on a baking sheet with the butternut squash and brush the squash with 15ml/1 tbsp of the remaining olive oil. Add the tomatoes, red pepper and fresh chilli for the salsa.

2 Roast the vegetables for 25 minutes, then remove the tomatoes, pepper and chilli. Reduce the temperature to 190°C/375°F/Gas 5 and cook the squash and garlic for 20–25 minutes more, or until the squash is tender.

3 Heat the remaining oil in a large, heavy pan and cook the onions and ground coriander gently for about 10 minutes, or until softened.

4 Skin the pepper and chilli and process in a food processor or blender with the tomatoes and 30ml/2 tbsp olive oil. Stir in the vinegar and seasoning to taste, adding a pinch of caster sugar. Add the remaining oil if you think the salsa needs it.

5 Squeeze the roasted garlic out of its papery skin into the onions and scoop the squash out of its skin, adding it to the pan. Add the stock, 5ml/1 tsp salt and plenty of black pepper. Bring to the boil and simmer for 10 minutes.

6 Stir in half the oregano or marjoram and cool the soup slightly, then process it in a blender or food processor. Alternatively, press the soup through a fine sieve (strainer).

7 Reheat the soup without allowing it to boil, then taste for seasoning before ladling it into warmed bowls. Top each with a spoonful of salsa and sprinkle over the remaining chopped oregano or marjoram. Serve immediately.

Energy 298Kcal/1245kJ; Protein 4.2g; Carbohydrate 26.7g, of which sugars 18g; Fat 20.3g, of which saturates 2.9g; Cholesterol 0mg; Calcium 118mg; Fibre 5.7g; Sodium 225mg.

MINESTRONE

THIS CLASSIC ITALIAN SOUP IS PACKED FULL OF VEGETABLES TO GIVE THE SYSTEM A VITAMIN BOOST AND HAS A FABULOUSLY STRONG FLAVOUR. IT'S HEARTY AND WARMING TOO.

SERVES FOUR TO SIX

INGREDIENTS
  1 onion
  2 celery sticks
  1 large carrot
  45ml/3 tbsp olive oil
  150g/5oz French (green) beans, cut
    into 5cm/2in pieces
  1 courgette (zucchini), thinly sliced
  1 potato, cut into 1cm/½in cubes
  ¼ Savoy cabbage, shredded
  1 small aubergine (eggplant), cut into
    1cm/½in cubes
  200g/7oz can cannellini beans,
    drained and rinsed
  2 Italian plum tomatoes, chopped
  1.2 litres/2 pints/5 cups stock
  90g/3½oz dried vermicelli
  salt and ground black pepper
For the pesto
  about 20 fresh basil leaves
  1 garlic clove
  10ml/2 tsp pine nuts
  15ml/1 tbsp grated Parmesan cheese
  15ml/1 tbsp grated Pecorino cheese
  30ml/2 tbsp olive oil

1 Chop the onion, celery and carrot finely, either in a food processor or by hand. Heat the oil in a large pan, add the chopped mixture and cook over a low heat, stirring frequently, for 5–7 minutes.

2 Mix in the French beans, courgette, potato and cabbage. Stir-fry over a medium heat for about 3 minutes. Add the aubergine, cannellini beans and tomatoes, and stir-fry for 2–3 minutes more. Pour in the stock with salt and pepper to taste. Bring to the boil. Stir well, cover and lower the heat. Simmer for 40 minutes, stirring occasionally.

3 Meanwhile, process all the pesto ingredients in a food processor until the mixture forms a smooth sauce, adding 15–45ml/1–3 tbsp water through the feeder tube if necessary.

4 Break the pasta into small pieces and add it to the soup. Simmer, stirring frequently, for 5 minutes. Add the pesto sauce and stir it in well, then simmer for 2–3 minutes more, or until the pasta is *al dente*. Taste for seasoning. Serve hot, in warmed soup plates or bowls.

Energy 387Kcal/1618kJ; Protein 13.1g; Carbohydrate 40g, of which sugars 9.6g; Fat 20.6g, of which saturates 4g; Cholesterol 8mg; Calcium 173mg; Fibre 7.7g; Sodium 527mg.

LEEK AND POTATO SOUP

ROCKET ADDS ITS DISTINCTIVE, PEPPERY TASTE TO THIS WONDERFULLY SATISFYING SOUP.
SERVE IT HOT, GARNISHED WITH A GENEROUS SPRINKLING OF TASTY CIABATTA CROÛTONS.

SERVES FOUR TO SIX

INGREDIENTS
50g/2oz/4 tbsp butter
1 onion, chopped
3 leeks, chopped
2 medium floury potatoes, diced
900ml/1½ pints/3¾ cups light
  chicken stock or water
2 large handfuls rocket (arugula),
  roughly chopped
150ml/¼ pint/⅔ cup double (heavy)
  cream
salt and ground black pepper
garlic-flavoured ciabatta croûtons,
  to serve

1 Melt the butter in a large heavy pan then add the onion, leeks and potatoes and stir until the vegetables are coated in butter. Heat the ingredients until sizzling then reduce the heat to low.

2 Cover and sweat the vegetables for 15 minutes. Pour in the stock or water and bring to the boil then reduce the heat, cover again and simmer for 20 minutes until the vegetables are tender.

3 Press the soup through a sieve (strainer) or pass through a food mill and return to the rinsed-out pan. (Don't use a blender or food processor, as these will give the soup a gluey texture.) Add the chopped rocket to the pan and cook the soup gently, uncovered, for 5 minutes.

4 Stir in the cream, then season to taste and reheat gently. Ladle the soup into warmed soup bowls and serve with a scattering of garlic-flavoured ciabatta croûtons in each.

Energy 385Kcal/1596kJ; Protein 5.3g; Carbohydrate 21.3g, of which sugars 5.4g; Fat 31.5g, of which saturates 19.2g; Cholesterol 78mg; Calcium 91mg; Fibre 4.4g; Sodium 282mg.

CHICKEN SOUP <u>WITH</u> DUMPLINGS

A BOWL OF CHICKEN SOUP CAN HEAL THE SOUL AS WELL AS THE BODY, AS ANYONE WHO HAS EVER SUFFERED FROM A HEAVY COLD OR FLU AND BEEN COMFORTED WILL KNOW.

<u>SERVES SIX TO EIGHT</u>

INGREDIENTS
1–1.5kg/2¼–3¼lb chicken, cut
   into portions
2–3 onions
3–4 litres/5–7 pints/12–16 cups
   water
3–5 carrots, thickly sliced
3–5 celery sticks, thickly sliced
1 small parsnip, cut in half
30–45ml/2–3 tbsp roughly chopped
   fresh parsley
30–45ml/2–3 tbsp chopped
   fresh dill
1–2 pinches ground turmeric
2 chicken stock (bouillon) cubes
2 garlic cloves, finely chopped
   (optional)
salt and ground black pepper
For the dumplings
   175g/6oz/¾ cup medium matzo meal
   2 eggs, lightly beaten
   45ml/3 tbsp vegetable oil or
      rendered chicken fat
   1 garlic clove, finely chopped
      (optional)
   30ml/2 tbsp chopped fresh parsley,
      plus extra to garnish
   ½ onion, finely grated
   1–2 pinches of chicken stock
      (bouillon) cube or powder (optional)
   about 90ml/6 tbsp water
   salt and ground black pepper

1 Put the chicken in a very large pan. Keeping them whole, cut a large cross in the stem end of each onion and add to the pan with the water, carrots, celery, parsnip, parsley, half the dill, the turmeric, and salt and black pepper.

2 Cover the pan and bring to the boil, then immediately lower the heat so that the liquid just simmers. Skim the soup and discard the scum that rises to the top. (Scum will continue to form but it is only the first scum that rises that will detract from the clarity and flavour of the soup.)

3 Add the crumbled stock cubes and simmer for 2–3 hours. When the chicken is cooked and the soup is well flavoured, remove the chicken pieces, and skim off the fat from the liquid surface. Alternatively, chill the soup and remove the layer of solid fat that forms.

4 To make the dumplings, in a large bowl combine the matzo meal with the eggs, oil or fat, chopped garlic, if using, parsley, onion, salt and pepper. Add only a little chicken stock cube or powder, if using, as these are salty. Add the water and mix together until the mixture is of the consistency of a thick, soft paste.

5 Cover the matzo batter and chill for 30 minutes, during which time the mixture will become firm.

6 Bring a pan of water to the boil and have a bowl of water next to the stove. Dip two tablespoons into the water, then take a spoonful of the matzo batter. With wet hands, roll it into a ball, then slip it into the boiling water and reduce the heat so that the water simmers. Continue with the remaining matzo batter, working relatively quickly, then cover the pan and cook for 15–20 minutes.

7 Remove the dumplings from the pan with a slotted spoon and transfer to a plate for about 20 minutes to firm up.

8 To serve, reheat the soup, adding the remaining dill and the garlic, if using. Put two to three dumplings in each bowl, pour over the hot soup and garnish.

VARIATIONS
• Instead of dumplings, the soup can be served over rice or noodles.
• To make lighter dumplings, separate the eggs and add the yolks to the matzo mixture. Whisk the whites until stiff then fold into the mixture.

Energy 449Kcal/1866kJ; Protein 27.4g; Carbohydrate 30g, of which sugars 6.2g; Fat 24.3g, of which saturates 5.4g; Cholesterol 186mg; Calcium 58mg; Fibre 2.9g; Sodium 399mg.

FRENCH COUNTRY OMELETTE

ALL OMELETTES ARE DELICIOUS AND CAN BE AS SUBSTANTIAL AS YOU WISH TO MAKE THEM BY ADDING FAVOURITE INGREDIENTS. THEY ARE ALSO PERFECT FOR SHARING.

SERVES TWO

INGREDIENTS

45–75ml/3–5 tbsp sunflower oil
50g/2oz thick bacon rashers (strips)
  or pieces, rinds removed and
  chopped
2 thick slices of bread, cut into
  small cubes
1 small onion, chopped
1–2 celery sticks, thinly sliced
115g/4oz cooked potato, diced
5 eggs, beaten
2 garlic cloves, crushed
handful of young spinach or sorrel
  leaves, stalks removed, torn
  into pieces
few sprigs of parsley, chopped
salt and ground black pepper

1 Heat the oil in a large heavy frying pan, and fry the bacon and bread cubes until they are crisp and turning golden. Add the chopped onion, celery and diced potato, and continue cooking slowly, stirring frequently until all the vegetables are soft and beginning to turn golden brown.

2 Beat the eggs with the garlic and seasoning, and pour over the vegetables. When the underside is beginning to set, add the spinach or sorrel. Cook until they have wilted and the omelette is only just soft in the middle. Fold the omelette in half and slide it out of the pan. Serve topped with the parsley, if liked.

Energy 549Kcal/2286kJ; Protein 27.1g; Carbohydrate 27.3g, of which sugars 3g; Fat 38.1g, of which saturates 8.2g; Cholesterol 584mg; Calcium 140mg; Fibre 1.9g; Sodium 770mg.

SPANISH OMELETTE

THE TRADITIONAL SPANISH OMELETTE CONSISTS SIMPLY OF POTATOES, ONIONS AND EGGS. THIS ONE ALSO HAS OTHER VEGETABLES AND WHITE BEANS. SERVE IT WITH A FRUITY RED WINE.

SERVES SIX

INGREDIENTS
    30ml/2 tbsp olive oil, plus extra
      for drizzling
    1 Spanish onion, chopped
    1 small red (bell) pepper, seeded
      and diced
    2 celery sticks, chopped
    225g/8oz potatoes, peeled, diced
      and cooked
    400g/14oz can cannellini
      beans, drained
    8 eggs
    salt and ground black pepper
    sprigs of oregano, to garnish
    green salad and olives, to serve

1 Heat the olive oil in a 30cm/12in non-stick or heavy frying pan until hot but not smoking. Add the onion, red pepper and celery, stir well and cook over medium heat for 3–5 minutes, stirring often, until the vegetables are soft, but not coloured.

2 Add the potato and beans, and cook, stirring or turning gently, for several minutes to heat through.

3 In a small bowl, beat the eggs with a fork, then season well and pour over the ingredients in the pan.

4 Stir until it begins to thicken, then allow it to cook over a low heat for about 8 minutes. The omelette should be firm, but still moist in the middle. Cool slightly then invert on to a serving plate.

5 Cut the omelette into thick wedges. Serve warm or cool with a green salad and olives and a little olive oil. Garnish with oregano.

COOK'S TIP
In Spain, this omelette is often served as a tapas dish or appetizer. It is delicious served cold, cut into bite-size pieces and accompanied with a chilli sauce or mayonnaise for dipping. Other sliced seasonal vegetables, baby artichoke hearts and chickpeas can also be used in this recipe.

Energy 253Kcal/1059kJ; Protein 15.5g; Carbohydrate 20g, of which sugars 4.8g; Fat 13.2g, of which saturates 3.1g; Cholesterol 304mg; Calcium 74mg; Fibre 4.6g; Sodium 403mg.

CHEESE AND ONION FLAN

BAKING SAVOURY TARTS IS JUST AS SATISFYING AS MAKING BUNS AND CAKES. MADE WITH YEAST DOUGH, THIS FRENCH CLASSIC IS GREAT FOR KNEADING OUT TENSIONS AND TROUBLES.

SERVES FOUR

INGREDIENTS
15g/½oz/1 tbsp butter
1 onion, halved and sliced
2 eggs
250ml/8fl oz/1 cup single (light)
 cream
225g/8oz strong semi-soft cheese,
 rind removed (about 175g/6oz
 without rind), sliced
salt and ground black pepper
salad leaves, to serve
For the yeast dough
10ml/2 tsp active dried yeast
120ml/4fl oz/½ cup milk
5ml/1 tsp sugar
1 egg yolk
225g/8oz/2 cups plain (all-purpose)
 flour
2.5ml/½ tsp salt
50g/2oz/4 tbsp butter, softened

1 To make the dough, place the yeast in a bowl. Warm the milk in a small pan until it is at body temperature and stir into the yeast with the sugar. Continue stirring until the yeast has dissolved completely. Leave the yeast mixture to stand for about 3 minutes, then beat in the egg yolk.

COOK'S TIP
If you prefer to use easy-blend (rapid rise) yeast, omit step 1. Beat the egg yolk and milk together in a bowl. Add the dry yeast to the flour and salt in the food processor, and pulse to combine. Pour in the egg and milk mixture, and proceed with the recipe as normal.

2 Put the flour and salt in a food processor fitted with a metal blade, and pulse to combine. With the machine running, slowly pour in the yeast mixture. Scrape down the sides and continue processing for 2–3 minutes. Add the softened butter and process for another 30 seconds.

3 Transfer the dough to a lightly greased bowl. Cover the bowl with a dishtowel and allow to rise in a warm place for about 1 hour until the dough has doubled in bulk.

4 Remove the dough from the bowl and place on a lightly floured surface. Knock back (punch down) the dough. Sprinkle a little more flour on the work surface and roll out the dough to a 30cm/12in round.

5 Line a 23cm/9in flan tin (pan) or dish with the dough. Gently press it into the tin or dish and trim off any overhanging pieces, leaving a 3mm/⅛in rim around the flan case. Cover with a dish towel, set aside in a warm place and leave the dough to rise again for about 30 minutes, or until puffy.

6 Meanwhile, melt the butter in a heavy pan and add the onion. Cover the pan and cook over a medium-low heat for about 15 minutes, until softened, stirring occasionally. Remove the lid and continue cooking, stirring frequently, until the onion is very soft and caramelized.

7 Preheat the oven to 180°C/350°F/Gas 4. Beat together the eggs and cream. Season and stir in the cooked onion.

8 Arrange the cheese on the base of the flan case. Pour over the egg mixture and bake for 30–35 minutes until the base is golden and the centre is just set. Cool slightly on a wire rack and serve warm with salad leaves.

Energy 717Kcal/2990kJ; Protein 24.8g; Carbohydrate 50.6g, of which sugars 6.9g; Fat 46.5g, of which saturates 28.1g; Cholesterol 288mg; Calcium 350mg; Fibre 2.3g; Sodium 735mg.

SMOKED SALMON QUICHE WITH POTATO PASTRY

THE INGREDIENTS IN THIS LIGHT BUT RICHLY-FLAVOURED QUICHE PERFECTLY COMPLEMENT THE MELT-IN-THE-MOUTH PASTRY MADE WITH POTATOES.

SERVES SIX

INGREDIENTS

For the pastry

115g/4oz floury maincrop
   potatoes, diced
225g/8oz/2 cups plain (all-purpose)
   flour, sifted
115g/4oz/8 tbsp butter, diced
½ egg, beaten
10ml/2 tsp chilled water

For the filling

275g/10oz smoked salmon
6 eggs, beaten
150ml/¼ pint/⅔ cup full cream milk
300ml/½ pint/1¼ cups double
   (heavy) cream
30–45ml/2–3 tbsp chopped
   fresh dill
30ml/2 tbsp capers, chopped
salt and ground black pepper

1 Boil the potatoes in a large pan of lightly salted water for 15 minutes or until tender. Drain well in a colander and return to the pan. Mash the potatoes until smooth and set aside to cool completely.

VARIATIONS

These quantities can also be used to make six individual quiches. Prepare as above, but reduce the cooking time by about 15 minutes. For extra piquancy, sprinkle some finely grated fresh Parmesan cheese over the top of each quiche before baking.

2 Place the flour in a bowl and rub in the butter to form fine crumbs. Beat in the potatoes and egg. Bring the mixture together, adding chilled water if needed.

3 Roll the pastry out on a floured surface and use to line a deep 23cm/9in round, loose-based, fluted flan tin (pan). Chill for 1 hour.

4 Preheat the oven to 200°C/400°F/ Gas 6. Place a baking sheet in the oven to preheat it. Chop the salmon into bite-size pieces and set aside.

5 For the filling, beat the eggs, milk and cream together. Then stir in the dill and capers and season with pepper. Add the salmon and stir to combine.

6 Remove the pastry case from the fridge, prick the base well and pour the mixture into it. Bake on a baking sheet for 35–45 minutes until set and golden.

COOK'S TIPS

• To ensure the base cooks through it is vital to preheat a baking sheet in the oven first.
• Make the most of smoked salmon offcuts for this quiche, as they are much cheaper.
• Serve the quiche warm, when it is especially delicious with mixed salad leaves combined with some more dill.

Energy 698Kcal/2902kJ; Protein 24.8g; Carbohydrate 34.6g, of which sugars 2.8g; Fat 52.3g, of which saturates 29.3g; Cholesterol 355mg; Calcium 154mg; Fibre 1.4g; Sodium 1086mg.

BUBBLE AND SQUEAK

WHETHER YOU HAVE LEFTOVERS, OR COOK THIS OLD-FASHIONED CLASSIC FROM FRESH, BE SURE TO GIVE IT A REALLY GOOD "SQUEAK" (FRY) IN THE PAN SO THAT ALL THE FLAVOURS CARAMELIZE.

SERVES FOUR

INGREDIENTS
  60ml/4 tbsp dripping, bacon fat or
    vegetable oil
  1 onion, finely chopped
  450g/1lb floury potatoes, cooked
    and mashed
  225g/8oz cooked cabbage or Brussels
    sprouts, finely chopped
  salt and ground black pepper

1 Heat 30ml/2 tbsp of the dripping, fat or oil in a heavy-based frying pan. Add the onion and cook, stirring frequently, until softened but not browned.

2 In a large bowl, mix together the potatoes and cooked cabbage or sprouts and season with salt and plenty of pepper to taste.

3 Add the vegetables to the pan with the cooked onions, stir well, then press the vegetable mixture into a large, even cake.

4 Cook over a medium heat for about 15 minutes until the cake is browned underneath.

5 Invert a large plate over the pan, and, holding it tightly against the pan, turn them both over together. Lift off the frying pan, return it to the heat and add the remaining dripping, fat or oil. When hot, slide the cake back into the pan, browned side uppermost.

6 Cook over a medium heat for 10 minutes or until the underside is golden brown. Serve hot, in wedges.

COOK'S TIP
If you don't have leftover cooked cabbage or Brussels sprouts, shred raw cabbage and cook with Brussels sprouts in boiling salted water until tender. Drain, then chop.

Energy 205Kcal/857kJ; Protein 3.5g; Carbohydrate 23.3g, of which sugars 4.2g; Fat 11.5g, of which saturates 1.2g; Cholesterol 0mg; Calcium 34mg; Fibre 3g; Sodium 15mg.

MUSHROOM PILAU

THIS DISH IS SIMPLICITY ITSELF. HERBS AND SPICES IMPART AN AROMATIC FLAVOUR, AND THE RICE MAKES A SATISFYING MEAL THAT IS PERFECT FOR A QUICK AND EASY SUPPER.

SERVES FOUR

INGREDIENTS
  30ml/2 tbsp vegetable oil
  2 shallots, finely chopped
  1 garlic clove, crushed
  3 green cardamom pods
  25g/1oz/2 tbsp ghee or butter
  175g/6oz/2½ cups button (white)
    mushrooms, sliced
  225g/8oz/generous 1 cup basmati
    rice, soaked
  5ml/1 tsp grated fresh root ginger
  good pinch of garam masala
  450ml/¾ pint/scant 2 cups water
  15ml/1 tbsp chopped fresh coriander
    (cilantro)
  salt

1 Heat the oil in a flameproof casserole and fry the shallots, garlic and cardamoms for 3–4 minutes until the shallots are beginning to brown.

2 Add the ghee or butter, then the mushrooms and fry for 2–3 minutes.

3 Add the rice, ginger and garam masala. Stir-fry over a low heat for 2–3 minutes, then stir in the water and a little salt. Bring to the boil, then cover tightly and simmer over a very low heat for 10 minutes.

4 Remove the casserole from the heat. Leave the pilau to stand, covered, for 5 minutes to complete the cooking. Add the chopped coriander and fork it through the rice. Spoon into a serving bowl and serve at once.

Energy 306Kcal/1273kJ; Protein 5.2g; Carbohydrate 45.5g, of which sugars 0.5g; Fat 11.2g, of which saturates 4g; Cholesterol 13mg; Calcium 17mg; Fibre 0.7g; Sodium 41mg.

TWO CHEESE RISOTTO

THIS UNDENIABLY RICH AND CREAMY RISOTTO IS JUST THE THING TO SERVE ON COLD WINTER EVENINGS WHEN EVERYONE NEEDS WARMING UP AND CHEERING UP.

SERVES THREE TO FOUR

INGREDIENTS

7.5ml/1½ tsp olive oil
50g/2oz/4 tbsp butter
1 onion, finely chopped
1 garlic clove, crushed
275g/10oz/1½ cups risotto rice,
    preferably Vialone Nano
175ml/6 fl oz/¾ cup dry white wine
1 litre/1¾ pints/4 cups simmering
    vegetable or chicken stock
75g/3oz/¾ cup Fontina cheese,
    cubed
50g/2oz/⅔ cup freshly grated
    Parmesan cheese, plus extra,
    to serve
salt and freshly ground black pepper

1 Heat the olive oil with half the butter in a pan and gently fry the onion and garlic for 5–6 minutes until soft. Add the rice and cook, stirring all the time, until the grains are coated in fat and have become slightly translucent around the edges.

2 Stir in the wine. Cook, stirring, until the liquid has been absorbed, then add a ladleful of hot stock. Stir until the stock has been absorbed, then add the remaining stock in the same way, waiting for each quantity of stock to be absorbed before adding more.

3 When the rice is half cooked, stir in the Fontina cheese, and continue cooking and adding stock. Keep stirring the rice all the time.

4 When the risotto is creamy and the grains are tender but still have a bit of "bite", stir in the remaining butter and the Parmesan. Season, then remove the pan from the heat, cover and leave to rest for 3–4 minutes before serving.

Energy 688Kcal/2863kJ; Protein 19.4g; Carbohydrate 77.7g, of which sugars 3.3g; Fat 28.2g, of which saturates 16.9g; Cholesterol 75mg; Calcium 304mg; Fibre 0.7g; Sodium 697mg.

QUICK RISOTTO

THIS IS RATHER A CHEAT'S RISOTTO AS IT DEFIES ALL THE RULES THAT INSIST THE STOCK IS ADDED GRADUALLY. INSTEAD, THE RICE IS COOKED QUICKLY IN A CONVENTIONAL WAY, AND THE OTHER INGREDIENTS ARE SIMPLY THROWN IN AT THE LAST MINUTE. IT TASTES GOOD FOR ALL THAT.

SERVES THREE TO FOUR

INGREDIENTS

275g/10oz/1½ cups risotto rice
1 litre/1¾ pints/4 cups simmering
    chicken stock
115g/4oz/1 cup mozzarella cheese,
    cut into small cubes
2 egg yolks
30ml/2 tbsp freshly grated Parmesan
    cheese
75g/3oz cooked ham, cut into
    small cubes
30ml/2 tbsp chopped fresh parsley
salt and freshly ground black pepper
fresh parsley sprigs, to garnish
freshly grated Parmesan cheese,
    to serve

1 Put the rice in a pan. Pour in the stock, bring to the boil and then cover and simmer for about 18–20 minutes until the rice is tender.

2 Remove the pan from the heat and quickly stir in the mozzarella, egg yolks, Parmesan, ham and parsley. Season well with salt and pepper.

3 Cover the pan and stand for 2–3 minutes to allow the cheese to melt, then stir again. Pile into warmed serving bowls, garnish and serve immediately, with extra Parmesan cheese.

Energy 544Kcal/2271kJ; Protein 24.6g; Carbohydrate 73.6g, of which sugars 0.3g; Fat 16.3g, of which saturates 8.6g; Cholesterol 181mg; Calcium 296mg; Fibre 0g; Sodium 838mg.

CHINESE FRIED RICE

THIS DISH IS QUICK, SIMPLE AND INEXPENSIVE; MOST IMPORTANTLY, IT IS ALSO EXTREMELY TASTY AND SATISFYING. ENJOY IT WITH A BOTTLE OF WINE.

SERVES FOUR

INGREDIENTS
    50g/2oz cooked ham
    50g/2oz cooked prawns (shrimp)
    3 eggs
    5ml/1 tsp salt
    2 spring onions (scallions), finely
      chopped
    60ml/4 tbsp vegetable oil
    115g/4oz/1 cup green peas, thawed
      if frozen
    15ml/1 tbsp light soy sauce
    15ml/1 tbsp Chinese rice wine or
      dry sherry
    450g/1lb/4 cups cooked white long
      grain rice

1 Dice the cooked ham finely. Pat the cooked prawns dry on kitchen paper.

2 In a bowl, beat the eggs with a pinch of salt and a few spring onion pieces.

VARIATIONS
Use cooked chicken or turkey instead of the ham, doubling the quantity if you omit the prawns.

3 Heat about half the oil in a wok, stir-fry the peas, prawns and ham for 1 minute, then add the soy sauce and rice wine or sherry. Transfer to a bowl and keep hot.

4 Heat the remaining oil in the wok and scramble the eggs lightly. Add the rice and stir to make sure that the grains are separate. Add the remaining salt, the remaining spring onions and the prawn mixture. Toss over the heat to mix. Serve hot or cold.

Energy 371Kcal/1552kJ; Protein 15.2g; Carbohydrate 38.9g, of which sugars 1.5g; Fat 18.4g, of which saturates 3.1g; Cholesterol 203mg; Calcium 71mg; Fibre 1.6g; Sodium 997mg.

THAI FRIED RICE

THIS SUBSTANTIAL DISH IS BASED ON THAI FRAGRANT RICE, WHICH IS SOMETIMES KNOWN AS JASMINE RICE. CHICKEN, RED PEPPER AND SWEETCORN ADD COLOUR AND EXTRA FLAVOUR.

SERVES FOUR

INGREDIENTS

475ml/16fl oz/2 cups water
50g/2oz/½ cup coconut milk powder
350g/12oz/1¾ cups Thai fragrant rice, rinsed
30ml/2 tbsp groundnut (peanut) oil
2 garlic cloves, chopped
1 small onion, finely chopped
2.5cm/1in piece of fresh root ginger, grated
225g/8oz skinless, boneless chicken breasts, cut into 1cm/½in dice
1 red (bell) pepper, seeded and sliced
115g/4oz/1 cup corn
5ml/1 tsp chilli oil
5ml/1 tsp hot curry powder
2 eggs, beaten
salt
spring onions (scallions), to garnish

3 Push the vegetables to the sides of the wok, add the chicken to the centre and stir-fry for 2 minutes until it is just cooked. Add the rice and stir-fry over a high heat for about 3 minutes more, until properly reheated.

4 Stir in the sliced red pepper, corn, chilli oil and curry powder, with salt to taste. Toss over the heat for 1 minute. Stir in the beaten eggs and cook for 1 minute more. Garnish with spring onion shreds and serve.

1 Pour the water into a pan and whisk in the coconut milk powder. Add the rice and bring to the boil. Lower the heat, cover and cook for 12 minutes or until the rice is tender and the liquid has been absorbed. Spread the rice on a baking sheet and leave until cold.

2 Heat the oil in a wok, add the garlic, onion and ginger and stir-fry over a medium heat for 2 minutes.

COOK'S TIP
It is important that the rice is completely cold before being fried and the oil is very hot, or the rice will absorb too much oil.

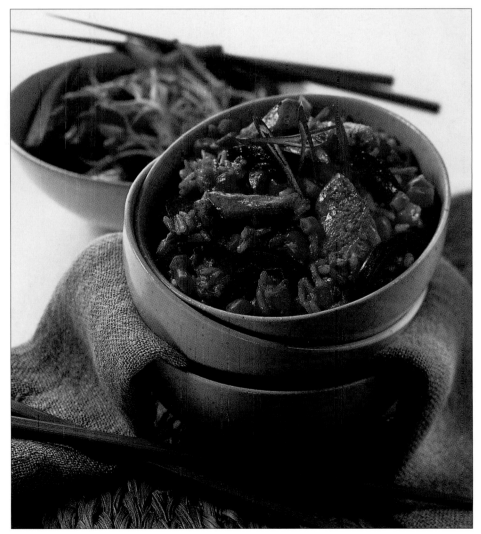

Energy 540Kcal/2282kJ; Protein 25.5g; Carbohydrate 84.7g, of which sugars 4.2g; Fat 13.5g, of which saturates 3.1g; Cholesterol 245mg; Calcium 73mg; Fibre 1.9g; Sodium 523mg.

SPICY FRIED NOODLES

THIS IS A WONDERFULLY VERSATILE DISH AS YOU CAN ADJUST IT TO INCLUDE YOUR FAVOURITE INGREDIENTS — JUST AS LONG AS YOU KEEP A BALANCE OF FLAVOURS, TEXTURES AND COLOURS.

SERVES FOUR

INGREDIENTS

    225g/8oz egg thread noodles
    60ml/4 tbsp vegetable oil
    2 garlic cloves, finely chopped
    175g/6oz pork fillet (tenderloin),
        sliced into thin strips
    1 skinless, boneless chicken breast
        portion (about 175g/6oz), sliced
        into thin strips
    115g/4oz/1 cup peeled cooked
        prawns (shrimp), rinsed if canned
    45ml/3 tbsp fresh lemon juice
    45ml/3 tbsp Thai fish sauce
    30ml/2 tbsp soft light brown sugar
    2 eggs, beaten
    ½ fresh red chilli, seeded and finely
        chopped
    50g/2oz/⅔ cup beansprouts
    60ml/4 tbsp roasted peanuts,
        chopped
    3 spring onions (scallions), cut into
        5cm/2in lengths and shredded
    45ml/3 tbsp chopped fresh coriander
        (cilantro)

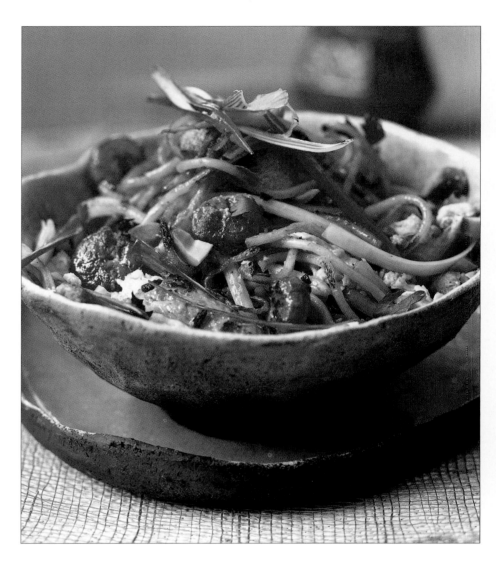

1 Bring a large pan of water to the boil. Add the noodles, remove the pan from the heat and leave for 5 minutes

2 Meanwhile, heat 45ml/3 tbsp of the oil in a wok or large frying pan, add the garlic and cook for 30 seconds. Add the pork and chicken and stir-fry until lightly browned, then add the prawns and stir-fry for 2 minutes.

4 Drain the noodles and add to the wok or pan with the remaining 15ml/1 tbsp oil. Toss all the ingredients together.

6 Divide the roasted peanuts, spring onions and coriander leaves into two equal portions, add one portion to the pan and stir-fry for about 2 minutes.

7 Place the noodles on a serving platter. Sprinkle on the remaining roasted peanuts, spring onions and chopped coriander and serve immediately.

COOK'S TIP
Store beansprouts in the refrigerator and use within a day of purchase, as they tend to lose their crispness and become slimy and unpleasant quite quickly. The most commonly used beansprouts are sprouted mung beans, but you could use other types of beansprouts instead.

3 Stir in the lemon juice, then add the fish sauce and sugar. Stir-fry until the sugar has dissolved.

5 Pour the beaten eggs over the noodles and stir fry until almost set, then add the chilli and beansprouts.

Energy 610Kcal/2560kJ; Protein 39.9g; Carbohydrate 52.4g, of which sugars 12g; Fat 28.3g, of which saturates 5.6g; Cholesterol 245mg; Calcium 78mg; Fibre 2.8g; Sodium 523mg.

SICHUAN NOODLES

FLAVOUR IS AN ALL-IMPORTANT FEATURE OF COMFORT MEALS. THOSE THAT ARE NOT FAMILIAR FROM CHILDHOOD AT LEAST HAVE TO BE SUFFICIENTLY PUNCHY AND DELICIOUS TO FILL THE SENSES WITH THE JOY OF EATING. THIS IS ONE OF THOSE DISHES AND IT IS ALSO SUPER-QUICK TO MAKE.

SERVES FOUR

INGREDIENTS

450g/1lb fresh or 225g/8oz dried
  egg noodles
½ cucumber, sliced lengthways,
  seeded and diced
4–6 spring onions (scallions)
a bunch of radishes, about 115g/4oz
225g/8oz mooli (daikon), peeled
115g/4oz/2 cups beansprouts, rinsed,
  then left in iced water and drained
60ml/4 tbsp groundnut (peanut) oil
  or sunflower oil
2 garlic cloves, crushed
45ml/3 tbsp toasted sesame paste
15ml/1 tbsp sesame oil
15ml/1 tbsp light soy sauce
5–10ml/1–2 tsp chilli sauce, to taste
15ml/1 tbsp rice vinegar
120ml/4 fl oz/½ cup chicken stock
  or water
5ml/1 tsp sugar, or to taste
salt and ground black pepper
roasted peanuts or cashew nuts,
  to garnish

1 If using fresh noodles, cook them in boiling water for 1 minute then drain well. Rinse the noodles in fresh water and drain again. Cook dried noodles according to the instructions on the packet, draining and rinsing them as for fresh noodles.

2 Place the cucumber in a colander or sieve, sprinkle with salt and leave to drain over a bowl for 15 minutes, rinse well, then drain and pat dry on kitchen paper. Place in a large salad bowl.

3 Cut the spring onions into fine shreds. Cut the radishes in half and slice finely. Coarsely grate the mooli using a mandolin or a food processor. Add all the vegetables to the cucumber and toss gently.

4 Heat half the oil in a wok or frying pan and stir-fry the noodles for about 1 minute. Using a slotted spoon, transfer the noodles to a large serving bowl and keep warm.

5 Add the remaining oil to the wok. When it is hot, fry the garlic to flavour the oil. Remove from the heat and stir in the sesame paste, with the sesame oil, soy and chilli sauces, vinegar and stock or water. Add a little sugar and season to taste. Warm through over a gentle heat. Do not overheat or the sauce will thicken too much. Pour the sauce over the noodles and toss well. Garnish with peanuts or cashew nuts and serve with the vegetables.

Energy 499Kcal/2088kJ; Protein 11.8g; Carbohydrate 60.3g, of which sugars 7.1g; Fat 25g, of which saturates 5.3g; Cholesterol 23mg; Calcium 85mg; Fibre 4.5g; Sodium 510mg.

PASTA WITH PESTO

BOTTLED PESTO IS A USEFUL STAND-BY, BUT IT BEARS NO RESEMBLANCE TO THE HEADY AROMA AND FLAVOUR OF THE FRESH PASTE. IT IS QUICK AND EASY TO MAKE IN A FOOD PROCESSOR.

SERVES FOUR

INGREDIENTS

50g/2oz/1⅓ cups fresh basil leaves,
  plus extra, to garnish
2–4 garlic cloves
60ml/4 tbsp pine nuts
120ml/4fl oz/½ cup extra virgin
  olive oil
115g/4oz/1⅓ cups freshly grated
  Parmesan cheese, plus extra
  to serve
25g/1oz/⅓ cup freshly grated
  Pecorino cheese
400g/14oz/3½ cups dried pasta
salt and ground black pepper

1 Put the basil leaves, garlic and pine nuts in a blender or food processor. Add 60ml/4 tbsp of the olive oil. Process until the ingredients are finely chopped, then stop the machine, remove the lid and scrape down the sides of the bowl.

2 Turn the machine on again and slowly pour the remaining oil in a thin, steady stream through the feeder tube. You may need to stop the machine and scrape down the sides of the bowl once or twice to make sure everything is evenly mixed.

3 Scrape the mixture into a large bowl and beat in the cheeses with a wooden spoon. Taste and add salt and pepper if necessary.

4 Cook the pasta according to the instructions on the packet. Drain it well, then add it to the bowl of pesto and toss well. Serve immediately, garnished with the fresh basil leaves. Hand shaved Parmesan around separately.

COOK'S TIP
Pesto can be made up to 2–3 days in advance. To store pesto, transfer it to a small bowl and pour a thin film of olive oil over the surface. Cover the bowl tightly with clear film and keep it in the refrigerator.

Energy 713Kcal/2969kJ; Protein 24.1g; Carbohydrate 43.2g, of which sugars 2.7g; Fat 50.5g, of which saturates 11.6g; Cholesterol 35mg; Calcium 468mg; Fibre 2.1g; Sodium 385mg.

CREAM FETTUCINE

THIS SIMPLE RECIPE WAS INVENTED BY A ROMAN RESTAURATEUR CALLED ALFREDO, WHO BECAME FAMOUS FOR SERVING IT WITH A GOLD FORK AND SPOON.

SERVES FOUR

INGREDIENTS
    50g/2oz/¼ cup butter
    200ml/7fl oz/scant 1 cup double
      (heavy) cream
    50g/2 oz/⅔ cup freshly grated
      Parmesan cheese, plus extra to serve
    350g/12oz fresh fettucine
    salt and freshly ground black pepper

COOK'S TIP
When you find a source of really good fresh pasta, buy some as an emergency ingredient and freeze it for future use. Spread it out thinly in a packet for freezing, if possible, so that it thaws quickly. Cook it from frozen and allow 1–2 minutes extra cooking time.

1 Melt the butter in a large pan. Add the cream and bring it to the boil. Simmer for 5 minutes, stirring constantly, then add the Parmesan cheese, with salt and freshly ground black pepper to taste, and turn off the heat under the pan.

2 Bring a large pan of salted water to the boil. Drop in the pasta all at once and quickly bring the water back to the boil, stirring occasionally. Cook for 2–3 minutes, or according to the instructions on the packet. Drain well.

3 Turn on the heat under the pan of cream to low, add the cooked pasta all at once and toss until it is thoroughly coated in the sauce. Taste the sauce for seasoning. Serve immediately, with extra grated Parmesan handed around separately.

COOK'S TIP
Cartons of long-life cream are invaluable for this recipe.

Energy 697Kcal/2912kJ; Protein 16.3g; Carbohydrate 65.8g, of which sugars 3.8g; Fat 42.8g, of which saturates 26g; Cholesterol 108mg; Calcium 199mg; Fibre 2.6g; Sodium 226mg.

MIXED MEAT CANNELLONI

A CREAMY, RICH FILLING AND SAUCE MAKE THIS AN UNUSUAL CANNELLONI — IT IS SERIOUSLY GOOD.

SERVES FOUR

INGREDIENTS

  60ml/4 tbsp olive oil
  1 onion, finely chopped
  1 carrot, finely chopped
  2 garlic cloves, crushed
  2 ripe Italian plum tomatoes, peeled
    and finely chopped
  130g/4½oz minced (ground) beef
  130g/4½oz minced pork
  250g/9oz minced chicken
  30ml/2 tbsp brandy
  25g/1oz/2 tbsp butter
  90ml/6 tbsp *panna da cucina* or
    double (heavy) cream
  16 dried cannelloni tubes
  75g/3oz/1 cup freshly grated
    Parmesan cheese
  salt and ground black pepper
  green salad, to serve
For the white sauce
  50g/2oz/¼ cup butter
  50g/2oz/½ cup plain (all-purpose)
    flour
  900ml/1½ pints/3¾ cups milk
  nutmeg

1 Heat the oil in a frying pan, add the onion, carrot, garlic and tomatoes and cook over a low heat, stirring, for about 10 minutes or until very soft.

COOK'S TIP

Sheets of fresh lasagne can be used instead of cannelloni tubes. Spoon some of the meat mixture at one end of a piece of lasagne and roll up, then place in the dish.

2 Add all the minced meats to the pan and cook gently for about 10 minutes, stirring frequently to break up any lumps of meat.

3 Pour in the brandy, increase the heat and boil, stirring, until it has reduced. Then add the butter and cream and cook gently, stirring occasionally, for about 10 minutes, until the mixture is rich and well cooked. Allow to cool.

4 Preheat the oven to 190°C/375°F/ Gas 5. Make the white sauce. Melt the butter in a medium pan, add the flour and cook, stirring, for 1–2 minutes. Add the milk a little at a time, whisking vigorously after each addition. Bring to the boil and cook, stirring, until the sauce is smooth and thick. Grate in nutmeg to taste, add salt and pepper and whisk. Remove from the heat.

5 Spoon a little of the white sauce into a baking dish. Fill the cannelloni tubes with the meat mixture and place in a single layer in the dish. Pour the remaining white sauce over them, then sprinkle with the Parmesan. Bake for 35–40 minutes or until the pasta feels tender when pierced with a skewer. Allow to stand for 10 minutes before serving with green salad.

Energy 1029Kcal/4304kJ; Protein 52.7g; Carbohydrate 72.3g, of which sugars 17.6g; Fat 59.1g, of which saturates 28.9g; Cholesterol 188mg; Calcium 568mg; Fibre 3.6g; Sodium 521mg.

SPAGHETTI BOLOGNESE

THIS RECIPE WILL BRING BACK HAPPY MEMORIES OF FLAT-SHARING AND COMMUNAL EATING.

SERVES FOUR TO SIX

INGREDIENTS

30ml/2 tbsp olive oil
1 onion, finely chopped
1 garlic clove, crushed
5ml/1 tsp dried mixed herbs
1.25ml/¼ tsp cayenne pepper
350–450g/12oz–1lb minced
  (ground) beef
400g/14oz can chopped Italian
  plum tomatoes
45ml/3 tbsp tomato ketchup
15ml/1 tbsp sun-dried tomato paste
5ml/1 tsp Worcestershire sauce
5ml1 tsp dried oregano
450ml/¾ pint/1¾ cups beef or
  vegetable stock
45ml/3 tbsp red wine
400–450g/14oz–1lb dried spaghetti
salt and ground black pepper
freshly grated Parmesan cheese,
  to serve

1 Heat the oil in a medium pan, add the onion and garlic and cook over a low heat, stirring frequently, for about 5 minutes until softened. Stir in the mixed herbs and cayenne and cook for 2–3 minutes more. Add the minced beef and cook gently for about 5 minutes, stirring frequently and breaking up any lumps in the meat with a wooden spoon.

2 Stir in the canned tomatoes, ketchup, sun-dried tomato paste, Worcestershire sauce, oregano and plenty of black pepper. Pour in the stock and red wine and bring to the boil, stirring. Cover the pan, lower the heat and leave the sauce to simmer for 30 minutes, stirring occasionally.

3 Cook the pasta according to the instructions on the packet. Drain well and divide among warmed bowls. Taste the sauce and add a little salt if necessary, then spoon it on top of the pasta and sprinkle with a little grated Parmesan. Serve immediately, with grated Parmesan handed separately.

Energy 639Kcal/2692kJ; Protein 30.9g; Carbohydrate 83.5g, of which sugars 11.5g; Fat 21.7g, of which saturates 7.1g; Cholesterol 53mg; Calcium 59mg; Fibre 4.2g; Sodium 312mg.

RICOTTA AND FONTINA PIZZA

PIZZA IS ALWAYS COMFORTING. THE EARTHY FLAVOUR OF THE MUSHROOMS IS DELICIOUS WITH CHEESE.

MAKES FOUR

INGREDIENTS
  2.5ml/½ tsp active dried yeast
  pinch of granulated sugar
  450g/1lb/4 cups strong white
    bread flour
  5ml/1 tsp salt
  30ml/2 tbsp olive oil
For the tomato sauce
  400g/14oz can chopped tomatoes
  150ml/¼ pint/⅔ cup passata (bottled
    strained tomatoes)
  1 large garlic clove, finely chopped
  5ml/1 tsp dried oregano
  1 bay leaf
  10ml/2 tsp malt vinegar
  salt and freshly ground black pepper
For the topping
  30ml/2 tbsp olive oil
  1 garlic clove, finely chopped
  350g/12oz/4 cups mushrooms, sliced
  30ml/2 tbsp chopped fresh oregano,
    plus whole leaves to garnish
  250g/9oz/generous 1 cup ricotta
    cheese
  225g/8oz Fontina cheese, sliced

1 Make the dough. Put 300ml/½ pint/ 1¼ cups warm water in a measuring jug. Add the yeast and the sugar and leave for 5–10 minutes until frothy. Sift the flour and salt into a large bowl and make a well in the centre. Gradually pour in the yeast mixture and the olive oil. Mix to make smooth dough.

2 Knead on a lightly floured surface for about 10 minutes until smooth, springy and elastic. Place the dough in a floured bowl, cover and leave to rise in a warm place for 1½ hours.

3 Meanwhile, make the tomato sauce. Place all the ingredients in a pan, cover and bring to the boil. Lower the heat, remove the lid and simmer for 20 minutes, stirring occasionally, until reduced.

4 Make the topping. Heat the oil in a frying pan. Add the garlic and mushrooms, with salt and pepper to taste. Cook, stirring, for about 5 minutes or until the mushrooms are golden brown. Set aside.

5 Preheat the oven to 220°/425°F/ Gas 7. Brush four baking sheets with oil. Knead the dough for 2 minutes, then divide into four equal pieces. Roll out each piece to a 25cm/10in round and place on a baking sheet.

6 Spoon the tomato sauce over each dough round. Brush the edge with a little olive oil. Add the mushrooms, oregano and cheese. Bake for about 15 minutes until golden brown and crisp. Sprinkle the oregano leaves over.

Energy 749Kcal/3149kJ; Protein 30.8g; Carbohydrate 93.1g, of which sugars 7g; Fat 29.5g, of which saturates 15.7g; Cholesterol 84mg; Calcium 473mg; Fibre 5.4g; Sodium 1000mg.

HOT PEPPERONI PIZZA

THERE IS NOTHING MORE MOUTHWATERING THAN A FRESHLY BAKED PIZZA, STRAIGHT FROM THE OVEN.

SERVES FOUR

INGREDIENTS

225g/8oz/2 cups strong white
  bread flour
10ml/2 tsp easy-blend (rapid-rise)
  dried yeast
5ml/1 tsp granulated sugar
2.5ml/½ tsp salt
15ml/1 tbsp olive oil
175ml/6fl oz/¾ cup mixed lukewarm
  milk and water
400g/14oz can chopped tomatoes,
  strained
2 garlic cloves, crushed
5ml/1 tsp dried oregano
225g/8oz mozzarella cheese, grated
2 dried red chillies, crumbled
225g/8oz pepperoni, sliced
30ml/2 tbsp drained capers
fresh oregano, to garnish

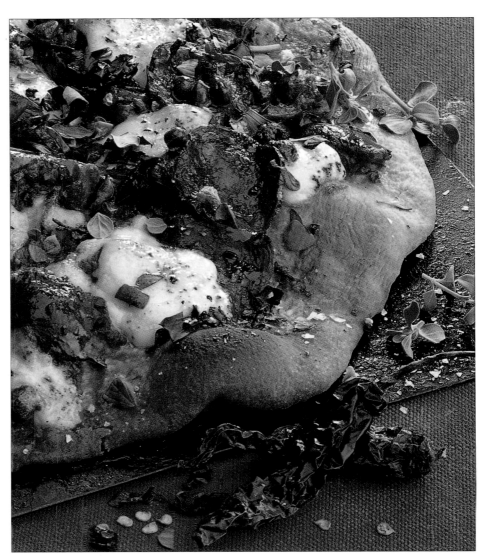

1 Sift the flour into a bowl. Stir in the yeast, sugar and salt. Make a well in the centre. Stir the olive oil into the milk and water, then stir the liquid into the flour. Mix to a soft dough.

2 Knead the dough on a lightly floured surface for 10 minutes until it is smooth and elastic. Cover and leave in a warm place for about 30 minutes or until the dough has doubled in bulk.

3 Preheat the oven to 220°C/425°F/ Gas 7. Turn the dough out on to a lightly floured surface and knead lightly for 1 minute. Divide it in half and roll each piece out to a 25cm/10in circle. Place on lightly oiled pizza trays or baking sheets.

4 To make the topping, mix the tomatoes, garlic and oregano in a bowl.

5 Spread half the tomato mixture over each base, leaving a border around the edge. Set half the mozzarella aside. Divide the rest between the pizzas.

6 Bake for 7–10 minutes until the dough rim on each pizza is pale golden.

7 Sprinkle the crumbled chillies over the pizzas, then arrange the pepperoni slices and capers on top. Sprinkle with the remaining mozzarella. Return the pizzas to the oven and bake for 7–10 minutes more. Sprinkle over the fresh oregano and serve at once.

Energy 556Kcal/2325kJ; Protein 24g; Carbohydrate 50.2g, of which sugars 5.2g; Fat 30.1g, of which saturates 12.7g; Cholesterol 136mg; Calcium 310mg; Fibre 2.7g; Sodium 992mg.

NO PLACE LIKE HOME

Every country has its classic recipes and every cook a favourite dish for nurturing their family and sharing with friends. This chapter offers a few examples of meals that have travelled far to become internationally appreciated. Classic Fish Pie, Green Chicken Curry with Coconut Rice, and Chicken Fajitas are a few favourites.

VEGETABLE MOUSSAKA

THIS CLASSIC GREEK DISH IS REALLY FLAVOURSOME. IT CAN BE SERVED WITH WARM FRESH BREAD FOR A HEARTY, SATISFYING MEAL THAT GIVES A GREAT SENSE OF HEALTHY EATING AND WELL-BEING.

SERVES SIX

INGREDIENTS

450g/1lb aubergines (eggplants),
  sliced
115g/4oz/½ cup whole green lentils
600ml/1 pint/2½ cups vegetable
  stock
1 bay leaf
45ml/3 tbsp olive oil
1 onion, sliced
1 garlic clove, crushed
225g/8oz/3 cups mushrooms, sliced
400g/14oz can chickpeas, rinsed
  and drained
400g/14oz can chopped tomatoes
30ml/2 tbsp tomato purée (paste)
10ml/2 tsp dried *herbes de Provence*
300ml/½ pint/1¼ cups natural
  (plain) yogurt
3 eggs
50g/2oz mature (sharp) Cheddar
  cheese, grated
salt and freshly ground black pepper
sprigs of fresh flat leaf parsley,
  to garnish

1 Sprinkle the aubergine slices with salt and place in a colander. Cover and place a weight on top. Leave for at least 30 minutes, to allow the bitter juices to be extracted.

2 Meanwhile, place the lentils, stock and bay leaf in a pan, cover, bring to the boil and simmer for about 20 minutes, until the lentils are just tender but not mushy. Add a little extra water if necessary. Drain thoroughly and keep warm.

3 Heat 15ml/1 tbsp of the oil in a large pan, add the onion and garlic and cook for 5 minutes, stirring. Stir in the lentils, mushrooms, chickpeas, tomatoes, tomato purée, herbs and 45ml/3 tbsp water. Bring to the boil, cover and simmer gently for 10–15 minutes, stirring from time to time.

4 Preheat the oven to 180°C/350°F/ Gas 4. Rinse the aubergine slices, drain and pat dry. Heat the remaining oil in a frying pan and fry the slices in batches for 3–4 minutes, turning once to brown both sides.

5 Season the lentil mixture with salt and pepper. Arrange a layer of aubergine slices in the bottom of a large, shallow, ovenproof dish or roasting tin, then spoon over a layer of the lentil mixture. Continue to build up the layers in this way until all the aubergine slices and lentil mixture are used up.

6 Beat the yogurt, eggs, salt and pepper together and pour the mixture over the dish. Sprinkle with the grated Cheddar cheese and bake for about 45 minutes, until the topping is golden brown and bubbling. Serve immediately, garnished with the flat leaf parsley.

VARIATION
Sliced and sautéed courgettes (zucchini) or potatoes can be used instead of the aubergines in this dish.

VEGETABLE KORMA

THE CAREFUL BLENDING OF SPICES IS WARMING AND STIMULATING IN TRADITIONAL INDIAN COOKING.
THIS KORMA DISH IS RICH, CREAMY AND SUBTLY FLAVOURED.

SERVES FOUR

INGREDIENTS

50g/2oz/¼ cup butter
2 onions, sliced
2 garlic cloves, crushed
2.5cm/1in piece fresh root
  ginger, grated
5ml/1 tsp ground cumin
15ml/1 tbsp ground coriander
6 cardamom pods
5cm/2in piece of cinnamon stick
5ml/1 tsp ground turmeric
1 fresh red chilli, seeded and
  finely chopped
1 potato, peeled and cut into
  2.5cm/1in cubes
1 small aubergine (eggplant),
  chopped
115g/4oz/1½ cups mushrooms,
  thickly sliced
175ml/6fl oz/¾ cup water
115g/4oz/1 cup green beans, cut into
  2.5cm/1in lengths
60ml/4 tbsp natural (plain) yogurt
150ml/¼ pint/⅔ cup double
  (heavy) cream
5ml/1 tsp garam masala
salt and ground black pepper
fresh coriander (cilantro) sprigs,
  to garnish
boiled rice and poppadums, to serve

1 Melt the butter in a heavy pan. Add the onions and cook for 5 minutes until soft. Add the garlic and ginger and cook for 2 minutes, then stir in the cumin, coriander, cardamom pods, cinnamon stick, turmeric and finely chopped chilli. Cook, stirring constantly, for 30 seconds.

2 Add the potato cubes, aubergine and mushrooms and the water. Cover the pan, bring to the boil, then lower the heat and simmer for 15 minutes. Add the beans and cook, uncovered, for 5 minutes. With a slotted spoon, remove the vegetables to a warmed serving dish and keep hot.

3 Increase the heat and allow the cooking liquid to bubble up until it has reduced a little. Season with salt and pepper, then stir in the yogurt, cream and garam masala. Pour the sauce over the vegetables and garnish with fresh coriander. Serve with boiled rice and crisp poppadums.

Energy 363Kcal/1499kJ; Protein 4.8g; Carbohydrate 16.6g, of which sugars 8.2g; Fat 31.3g, of which saturates 19.2g; Cholesterol 78mg; Calcium 88mg; Fibre 3.7g; Sodium 104mg.

LENTIL DHAL

THIS LENTIL DHAL MAKES A SUSTAINING AND COMFORTING MEAL WHEN SERVED WITH RICE OR INDIAN BREADS AND ANY DRY-SPICED DISH, PARTICULARLY A CAULIFLOWER OR POTATO DISH.

SERVES FOUR TO SIX

INGREDIENTS
40g/1½oz/3 tbsp butter or ghee
1 onion, chopped
2 green chillies, seeded and chopped
15ml/1 tbsp chopped fresh root
  ginger
225g/8oz/1 cup yellow or red lentils
900ml/1½ pints/3¾ cups water
45ml/3 tbsp roasted garlic purée
5ml/1 tsp ground cumin
5ml/1 tsp ground coriander
200g/7oz tomatoes, peeled and
  diced
a little lemon juice
salt and ground black pepper
30–45ml/2–3 tbsp coriander
  (cilantro) sprigs, to garnish
For the spicy garnish
30ml/2 tbsp groundnut (peanut) oil
4–5 shallots, sliced
2 garlic cloves, thinly sliced
15g/½oz/1 tbsp butter or ghee
5ml/1 tsp cumin seeds
5ml/1 tsp mustard seeds
3–4 small dried red chillies
8–10 fresh curry leaves

COOK'S TIP
Ghee is a type of clarified butter that has had all the milk solids and water removed by heating – it was originally made to extend the keeping qualities of butter in India. It is the main cooking fat used in traditional Indian cooking. Because the milk solids have been removed, ghee has a high smoking point and can therefore be cooked at higher temperatures than ordinary butter. Look for it in Indian and Asian stores or with specialist ranges in the supermarket.

1 First begin the spicy garnish. Heat the oil in a large, heavy pan. Add the shallots and fry them over a medium heat, stirring occasionally, until they are crisp and browned. Add the garlic and cook, stirring frequently, for a moment or two until the garlic colours slightly. Use a slotted spoon to remove the mixture from the pan and set aside.

2 Melt the butter or ghee in the pan and cook the onion, chillies and ginger for 10 minutes, until golden.

3 Stir in the lentils and water, then bring to the boil, reduce the heat and part-cover the pan. Simmer, stirring occasionally, for 50–60 minutes, until similar to a very thick soup.

4 Stir in the roasted garlic purée, cumin and ground coriander, then season with salt and pepper to taste. Cook for a further 10–15 minutes, uncovered, stirring frequently.

5 Stir in the tomatoes and then adjust the seasoning, adding a little lemon juice to taste if necessary.

6 To make the spicy garnish: melt the butter or ghee in a frying pan. Add the cumin and mustard seeds and fry until the mustard seeds pop. Stir in the chillies, curry leaves and the shallot mixture, then immediately swirl the mixture into the cooked dhal. Garnish with coriander, spicy fried shallots and garlic and serve.

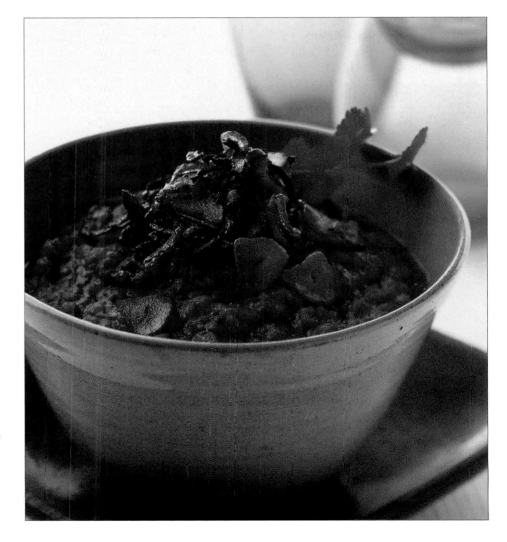

Energy 359Kcal/1502kJ; Protein 14.3g; Carbohydrate 36.3g, of which sugars 5.1g; Fat 18.4g, of which saturates 8.9g; Cholesterol 32mg; Calcium 43mg; Fibre 3.8g; Sodium 87mg.

SEAFOOD CHOWDER

LIKE MOST CHOWDERS, THIS DISH FROM NEW ENGLAND IS A SUBSTANTIAL, HOMELY DISH, WHICH IS DELICIOUS WITH CHUNKS OF GOOD CRUSTY BREAD.

SERVES FOUR TO SIX

INGREDIENTS

200g/7oz/generous 1 cup drained
  canned corn
600ml/1 pint/2½ cups milk
15g/½oz/1 tbsp butter
1 small leek, sliced
1 small garlic clove, crushed
2 rindless smoked streaky (fatty)
  bacon rashers (strips), finely
  chopped
1 small green or red (bell) pepper,
  seeded and diced
1 celery stick, chopped
115g/4oz/generous ½ cup white long
  grain rice
5ml/1 tsp plain (all-purpose) flour
about 450ml/¾ pint/scant 2 cups hot
  chicken or vegetable stock
4 large scallops
115g/4oz white fish fillet, such as
  monkfish, plaice or flounder
15ml/1 tbsp finely chopped fresh flat
  leaf parsley
good pinch of cayenne pepper
30–45ml/2–3 tbsp single (light)
  cream (optional)
salt and ground black pepper
crusty bread, to serve

VARIATIONS
• You can use other shellfish in place of the scallops if you prefer – try fresh or frozen prawns (shrimp), or mussels or clams, which are equally good in or out of their shells.
• Allow frozen shellfish to thaw at room temperature before adding to the chowder.
• Undyed, naturally smoked haddock or cod would make a delicious alternative fish.

1 Place half the drained corn in a food processor or blender. Add a little of the milk and then process until the mixture is thick and creamy. Set aside.

2 Melt the butter in a large, heavy pan. Add the leek, garlic and bacon and gently fry for 4–5 minutes until the leek has softened but not browned.

3 Add the diced green or red pepper and the chopped celery and cook over a very gentle heat for 3–4 minutes more, stirring frequently, until the pepper and celery have softened slightly.

4 Stir in the rice and cook for a few minutes, stirring occasionally, until the grains begin to swell, then sprinkle the flour evenly over the top of the rice and vegetables. Cook for about 1 minute, stirring all the time, then gradually stir in the remaining milk and the hot stock.

5 Bring the mixture to the boil over a medium heat, then lower the heat and stir in the creamed corn mixture, with the whole corn. Season well.

6 Cover the pan and simmer very gently for about 20 minutes, or until the rice is tender, stirring occasionally. Add a little more chicken or vegetable stock or water to the pan if the mixture thickens too quickly or if the rice begins to stick to the base of the pan.

7 Cut the corals away from the scallops and set them aside; slice the white flesh into 5mm/¼in pieces. Cut the white fish fillet into bitesize chunks.

8 Add the scallops and chunks of fish to the chowder. Stir gently, then cook for 4 minutes.

9 Stir in the scallop corals, parsley and cayenne pepper. Cook for a few minutes until the scallops are just cooked and heated through, then stir in the cream, if using. Adjust the seasoning and serve.

COOK'S TIP
Instead of using a food processor, chop the corn finely and transfer to a bowl. Beat in the milk a little at a time until the mixture is thick and creamy.

Energy 373Kcal/1569kJ; Protein 26g; Carbohydrate 45.1g, of which sugars 11.8g; Fat 10.4g, of which saturates 4.8g; Cholesterol 54mg; Calcium 217mg; Fibre 2.7g; Sodium 313mg.

CHICKEN FLAUTAS

CRISP FRIED MEXICAN TORTILLAS WITH A CHICKEN AND CHEESE FILLING MAKE A DELICIOUS MEAL, ESPECIALLY WHEN SERVED WITH A SPICY TOMATO SALSA. THE SECRET OF SUCCESS IS TO MAKE SURE THAT THE OIL IS SUFFICIENTLY HOT TO PREVENT THE FLUTES FROM ABSORBING TOO MUCH OF IT.

MAKES TWELVE

INGREDIENTS

2 skinless, boneless chicken breasts
1 onion
2 garlic cloves
15ml/1 tbsp vegetable oil
90g/3½oz feta cheese, crumbled
12 corn tortillas, freshly made or a
  few days old
oil, for frying
salt and ground black pepper
For the salsa
  3 tomatoes, peeled, seeded
    and chopped
  juice of ½ lime
  small bunch of fresh coriander
    (cilantro), chopped
  ½ small onion, finely chopped
  3 fresh fresno chillies or similar
    fresh green chillies, seeded
    and chopped

1 Start by making the salsa. Mix the tomatoes, lime juice, coriander, onion and chillies in a bowl. Season with salt to taste and set aside.

COOK'S TIP
You might find it easier to keep the cocktail sticks in place until after the flutes have been fried, in which case remove them before serving.

2 Put the chicken breasts in a large pan, add water to cover and bring to the boil. Lower the heat and simmer for 15–20 minutes or until the chicken is cooked. Remove the chicken from the pan and let it cool a little. Using two forks, shred the chicken into small pieces. Set it aside.

3 Chop the onion finely and crush the garlic. Heat the oil in a frying pan, add the onion and garlic and fry over a low heat for about 5 minutes, or until the onion has softened but not coloured. Add the shredded chicken, with salt and pepper to taste. Mix well, remove from the heat and stir in the feta.

4 Before they can be rolled, soften the tortillas by steaming three or four at a time on a plate over boiling water for a few moments until they are pliable. Alternatively, wrap them in microwave-safe film and then heat them in a microwave oven on full power for about 30 seconds.

5 Place a spoonful of the chicken filling on one of the tortillas. Roll the tortilla tightly around the filling to make a neat cylinder. Secure with a cocktail stick (toothpick). Cover the roll with clear film (plastic wrap) to prevent the tortilla from drying out and splitting. Fill the remaining tortillas in the same way.

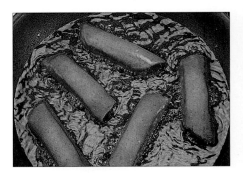

6 Pour oil into a frying pan to a depth of 2.5cm/1in. Heat it until a small cube of bread, added to the oil, rises to the surface and bubbles at the edges before turning golden. Remove the cocktail sticks, then add the flutes to the pan, a few at a time.

7 Fry the flutes for 2–3 minutes until golden, turning frequently. Drain on kitchen paper and serve at once, with the salsa.

Energy 89Kcal/374kJ; Protein 9.1g; Carbohydrate 6.9g, of which sugars 1.7g; Fat 2.9g, of which saturates 1.3g; Cholesterol 26mg; Calcium 43mg; Fibre 0.6g; Sodium 151mg.

CHICKEN FAJITAS

THE PERFECT DISH FOR CASUAL ENTERTAINING. IN MEXICO FAJITAS ARE FLOUR TORTILLAS THAT ARE BROUGHT TO THE TABLE FRESHLY COOKED. GUESTS ADD THEIR OWN FILLINGS BEFORE FOLDING THE TORTILLAS AND TUCKING IN. THIS IS DELICIOUSLY FUN FOOD FOR SOCIABLE DINING.

SERVES SIX

INGREDIENTS
    3 skinless, boneless chicken breasts
    finely grated rind and juice of
        2 limes
    30ml/2 tbsp caster (superfine) sugar
    10ml/2 tsp dried oregano
    2.5ml/½ tsp cayenne pepper
    5ml/1 tsp ground cinnamon
    2 onions
    3 (bell) peppers (1 red, 1 yellow or
        orange and 1 green)
    45ml/3 tbsp vegetable oil
    guacamole, salsa and sour cream,
        to serve
For the tortillas
    250g/9oz/2¼ cups plain (all-purpose)
        flour, sifted
    1.5ml/¼ tsp baking powder
    pinch of salt
    50g/2oz/¼ cup lard (shortening) or
        white cooking fat
    60ml/4 tbsp warm water

1 Slice the chicken breasts into 2cm/¾in wide strips and place these in a large bowl. Add the lime rind and juice, caster sugar, oregano, cayenne and cinnamon. Mix thoroughly. Set aside to marinate for at least 30 minutes.

COOK'S TIP
Tortilla dough can be very difficult to roll out thinly. If the dough is breaking up try placing each ball between two sheets of clean plastic (this can be cut from a new sandwich bag). Roll out, turning over, still inside the plastic, until the tortilla is the right size.

2 Meanwhile, make the tortillas. Mix the flour, baking powder and salt in a large bowl. Rub in the lard, then add the warm water, a little at a time, to make a stiff dough. Knead this on a lightly floured surface for 10–15 minutes until it is smooth and elastic.

3 Divide the dough into 12 small balls, then roll each into a 15cm/6in round. Cover the rounds with plastic or clear film (plastic wrap) to stop them drying out while you prepare the vegetables.

4 Cut the onions in half and slice them thinly. Cut the peppers in half, remove the cores and seeds, then slice the flesh into 1cm/½in wide strips.

5 Heat a large frying pan or griddle and cook each tortilla in turn for about 1 minute on each side, or until the surface colours and begins to blister. Keep the cooked tortillas warm and pliable by wrapping them in a clean, dry dish towel.

6 Heat the oil in a large frying pan. Stir-fry the marinated chicken for 5–6 minutes, then add the peppers and onions and cook for 3–4 minutes more, until the chicken strips are cooked through and the vegetables are soft and tender, but still juicy.

7 Spoon the chicken mixture into a serving bowl and take it to the table with the cooked tortillas, guacamole, salsa and sour cream. Keep the tortillas wrapped and warm.

8 To serve, each guest takes a warm tortilla, spreads it with a little salsa, adds a spoonful of guacamole and piles some of the chicken mixture in the centre. The final touch is to add a small dollop of sour cream. The tortilla is then folded over the filling and eaten in the hand.

Energy 405Kcal/1698kJ; Protein 26.4g; Carbohydrate 41.9g, of which sugars 8.8g; Fat 15.7g, of which saturates 4.5g; Cholesterol 69mg; Calcium 82mg; Fibre 3.4g; Sodium 157mg.

GREEN CHICKEN CURRY <u>WITH</u> COCONUT RICE

THERE IS SOMETHING SATISFYING ABOUT COOKING A ONE-POT MEAL. PERHAPS IT'S BECAUSE IT TAKES NO EFFORT TO MAKE, OR MAYBE IT'S THE BLEND OF FLAVOURS THAT MAKES IT SO APPEALING.

SERVES THREE TO FOUR

INGREDIENTS

   4 spring onions (scallions), trimmed
      and roughly chopped
   1–2 fresh green chillies, seeded and
      roughly chopped
   2cm/¾in piece of fresh root
      ginger, peeled
   2 garlic cloves
   5ml/1 tsp Thai fish sauce
   large bunch of fresh coriander
      (cilantro)
   small handful of fresh parsley
   30–45ml/2–3 tbsp water
   30ml/2 tbsp sunflower oil
   4 skinless, boneless chicken
      breasts, cubed
   1 green (bell) pepper, seeded and
      finely sliced
   75g/3oz piece of creamed coconut
      dissolved in 400ml/14fl oz/1⅔ cups
      boiling water
   salt and freshly ground black pepper
For the rice
   225g/8oz/generous 1 cup Thai
      fragrant rice, rinsed
   75g/3oz piece of creamed coconut
      dissolved in 400ml/14fl oz/1⅔ cups
      boiling water
   1 lemon grass stalk, quartered and
      bruised

2 Heat half the oil in large frying pan. Fry the chicken cubes until evenly browned. Transfer to a plate.

3 Heat the remaining oil. Stir-fry the green pepper for 3–4 minutes, then add the chilli and ginger paste. Fry, stirring, for 3–4 minutes until the mixture becomes fairly thick.

5 When the chicken is cooked, transfer it with the peppers to a plate. Boil the cooking liquid remaining in the pan for 10–12 minutes until it is well reduced and fairly thick.

6 Meanwhile, put the rice in a large pan. Add the coconut liquid and the bruised pieces of lemon grass. Stir in a little salt, bring to the boil, then lower the heat, cover and simmer very gently for 10 minutes, or for the time recommended on the packet. When the rice is tender, discard the pieces of lemon grass and fork the rice on to a warmed serving plate.

7 Return the chicken and peppers to the green curry sauce, stir well and cook gently for a few minutes to heat through. Spoon the curry over the rice, and serve immediately.

1 Process the spring onions, chillies, ginger, garlic, fish sauce, fresh herbs and water to a smooth paste in a food processor or blender.

4 Return the chicken to the pan and add the coconut liquid. Season. Bring to the boil, lower the heat; half cover the pan and simmer for 8–10 minutes.

COOK'S TIP
If you cannot find creamed coconut, use 150ml/¼ pint/⅔ cup coconut milk and 250ml/8fl oz/1 cup water for the curry and the same quantities again for the rice.

Energy 699Kcal/2963kJ; Protein 65.4g; Carbohydrate 82.9g, of which sugars 18.2g; Fat 14.2g, of which saturates 3g; Cholesterol 163mg; Calcium 184mg; Fibre 3.2g; Sodium 448mg.

LASAGNE

THIS RICH ITALIAN LASAGNE IS MADE WITH GOOD HOME-MADE MEAT SAUCE AND A WHITE SAUCE LAYERED WITH FRESHLY GRATED PARMESAN CHEESE. KEEP THE LAYERS OF SAUCES THIN.

SERVES SIX

INGREDIENTS
   8–10 lasagne sheets, green or white
   75g/3oz/1 cup freshly grated
      Parmesan cheese
   salt and ground black pepper
   sprigs of flat leaf parsley, to garnish
For the meat sauce
   45ml/3 tbsp olive oil
   500g/1¼lb lean minced (ground)
      beef
   75g/3oz smoked bacon or
      pancetta, diced
   130g/4½oz chicken livers, trimmed
      and chopped (optional)
   1 onion, finely chopped
   2 garlic cloves, crushed
   150ml/¼ pint/⅔ cup dry white
      wine (optional)
   30–45ml/2–3 tbsp tomato purée
      (paste)
   2 x 400g/14oz cans chopped
      tomatoes
   45ml/3 tbsp single (light) cream
For the white sauce
   600ml/1 pint/2½ cups milk
   1 bay leaf
   1 small onion, sliced
   50g/2oz/¼ cup butter
   40g/1½oz/⅓ cup plain (all-purpose)
      flour
   freshly grated nutmeg

1 Bring a large pan of water to the boil and blanch the pasta sheets, a few at a time, for at least 2 minutes, taking care to keep them separate. Stir the pasta during cooking to stop it sticking. Drain the blanched sheets and set them aside in a bowl of cold water.

2 Make the meat sauce. Heat the oil in a large frying pan. Add the minced beef and cook, stirring, until it is evenly browned. Add the bacon or pancetta and chicken livers, if using, and cook for 3–4 minutes.

3 Add the onion and garlic. Cook for 5 minutes more, until the onion has softened slightly. Stir in the wine, if using. Bring to the boil and cook until well reduced.

4 Stir in the tomato purée and tomatoes, with salt and pepper to taste. Bring to the boil, then lower the heat and simmer for 15–20 minutes until thickened. Stir in the cream, if using, and set aside.

5 While the meat sauce is simmering, make the white sauce. Pour the milk into a pan and add the bay leaf and sliced onion. Heat gently until the milk is just below boiling point, then remove the pan from the heat and leave to infuse for 10 minutes. Strain the milk into a jug (pitcher) and discard the bay leaf and onion.

6 Melt the butter in a pan and stir in the flour. Cook for 1 minute, stirring, then gradually whisk in the milk until the mixture boils and thickens to a smooth sauce. Season and add nutmeg to taste.

7 Drain the pasta sheets and pat them dry on a clean dish towel or with kitchen paper. Lay them out to prevent them from sticking together.

8 Spread some meat sauce on the base of a rectangular baking dish. Top with a single layer of pasta sheets. Trickle over some white sauce and sprinkle with Parmesan. Repeat the layers until all the ingredients have been used, finishing with a layer made by swirling the last of the two sauces together. Sprinkle liberally with Parmesan.

9 Preheat the oven to 190°C/375°F/ Gas 5 and bake the lasagne for about 30 minutes until bubbling and golden brown. Allow to stand for 10 minutes before cutting. Serve garnished with flat leaf parsley.

Energy 586Kcal/2457kJ; Protein 40.5g; Carbohydrate 39.8g, of which sugars 11.2g; Fat 30.7g, of which saturates 13.5g; Cholesterol 175mg; Calcium 343mg; Fibre 1.6g; Sodium 606mg.

MOUSSAKA

THIS CLASSIC GREEK DISH WITH LAMB, POTATOES AND AUBERGINES IS LAYERED WITH A RICH CHEESY TOPPING TO MAKE A SUBSTANTIAL MEAL THAT IS IRRESISTIBLY GOOD WITH A CRISP SIDE SALAD.

SERVES SIX

INGREDIENTS
    30ml/2 tbsp olive oil
    30ml/2 tbsp chopped fresh oregano
    1 large onion, finely chopped
    675g/1½lb lean lamb, minced
      (ground)
    1 large aubergine (eggplant), sliced
    2 x 400g/14oz cans chopped
      tomatoes
    45ml/3 tbsp tomato purée (paste)
    1 lamb stock cube, crumbled
    2 floury main crop potatoes, halved
    115g/4oz/1 cup Cheddar cheese,
      grated
    150ml/¼ pint/⅔ cup single (light)
      cream
  salt and ground black pepper
  fresh bread, to serve

1 Preheat the oven to 180°C/350°F/ Gas 4. Heat the olive oil in a large deep-sided frying pan. Fry the oregano and onions over a low heat, stirring frequently, for about 5 minutes or until the onions have softened.

VARIATION
If you want to add more vegetables to the dish, use slices of courgette, grilled in the same way as the aubergines, instead of the sliced potato in the layers, then top the dish with a layer of well-seasoned mashed potatoes before pouring over the sauce. To make the dish even richer, add a sprinkling of freshly grated Parmesan cheese with each layer of aubergine.

2 Stir in the lamb and cook for 10 minutes until browned. Meanwhile, grill the aubergine slices for 5 minutes until browned, turning once.

3 Stir the tomatoes and purée into the lamb mixture, and crumble the stock cube over it, stir well, season with salt and pepper and simmer uncovered for a further 15 minutes.

4 Meanwhile, cook the potatoes in lightly salted boiling water for 5–10 minutes until just tender. Drain, and when cool enough to handle, cut into thin slices.

5 Layer the aubergines, lamb and potatoes in a 1.75 litre/3 pint/7½ cup oval ovenproof dish, finishing with a layer of potatoes.

6 Mix the cheese and cream together in a bowl and pour over the top of the other ingredients in the dish. Cook for 45–50 minutes until bubbling and golden on the top. Serve straight from the dish, while hot, with plenty of fresh, crusty bread.

COOK'S TIP
The larger the surface area of the dish, the quicker the moussaka will cook; however, the dish must be deep enough to hold the layers and allow the sauce to bubble up during baking without boiling over the rim.

Energy 465Kcal/1938kJ; Protein 30.5g; Carbohydrate 18.3g, of which sugars 7.4g; Fat 30.1g, of which saturates 14.7g; Cholesterol 119mg; Calcium 215mg; Fibre 2.8g; Sodium 281mg.

BLUES BUSTERS

When the pace of life brings on a session of singing the blues, kick-start a positive new attitude with a real meal. This chapter is full of fabulous dishes that make food worth eating and life worth living. There are classic casseroles, such as Fisherman's Stew and Traditional Beef Stew with Dumplings; aromatic roast lamb or chicken and steaming hot pies.

FISHERMAN'S STEW

LIGHT SEAFOOD IN A CREAMY SAUCE MAKES AN IRRESISTIBLE CASSEROLE TO CHEER DREARY DAYS. THIS IS ESPECIALLY GOOD WITH LOTS OF WARM CRUSTY BREAD TO MOP UP EVERY LAST DROP.

SERVES SIX

INGREDIENTS
500g/1¼lb mussels
3 onions
2 garlic cloves, sliced
300ml/½ pint/1¼ cups fish stock
12 scallops
450g/1lb cod fillet
30ml/2 tbsp olive oil
1 large potato, about 200g/7oz
few sprigs of fresh thyme, chopped
1 red and 1 green (bell) pepper
120ml/4fl oz/½ cup dry white wine
250ml/8fl oz/1 cup crème fraîche
275g/10oz raw peeled prawns
  (shrimp)
75g/3oz/¾ cup grated mature (sharp)
  Cheddar cheese
salt and ground black pepper
fresh thyme sprigs, to garnish

1 Clean the mussels, removing any beards. Discard any that stay open when tapped. Rinse in cold water.

2 Pour water into a large, frying pan to 2.5cm/1in. Chop an onion and add it to the pan, with the garlic. Bring to the boil, add the mussels and cover.

3 Cook the mussels for 5–6 minutes, shaking the pan occasionally. Remove them as they open, discarding any that remain shut. Remove the mussels from their shells and set them aside.

4 Strain the cooking liquid from the mussels through a muslin- (cheese-cloth-) lined sieve (strainer) to remove any sand. Make up the liquid with fish stock to 300ml/½ pint/1¼ cups.

5 If you have bought scallops in their shells, open them: hold a scallop shell in the palm of your hand, with the flat side uppermost. Insert the blade of a knife close to the hinge that joins the shells and prise apart. Run the blade of the knife across the inside of the flat shell to cut away the scallop. Only the white adductor muscle and the orange coral are eaten, so pull away and discard all other parts. Rinse the scallops under cold running water to remove any grit or sand, then put them in a bowl and set them aside.

6 Cut the cod into large cubes and put it in a bowl. Season with salt and pepper and set aside.

7 Cut the remaining onions into small wedges. Heat the olive oil in a large pan and fry the onion wedges for 2–3 minutes. Slice the potato about 1cm/½in thick and add to the pan, with the fresh chopped thyme. Cover and cook for about 15 minutes, until the potato has softened.

8 Core the peppers, remove the cores and seeds, then dice the flesh. Add to the onion and potato mixture and cook for a few minutes. Stir in the mixed mussel and fish stock, with the wine and crème fraîche.

9 Bring to just below boiling point, then add the cod and scallops. Lower the heat and simmer for 5 minutes, then add the prawns. Simmer for a further 3–4 minutes more, until all the seafood is cooked. Stir in the mussels and warm through for 1–2 minutes. Season the sauce if necessary. Spoon into bowls, garnish with the thyme sprigs and sprinkle with the cheese. Crusty bread is an ideal accompaniment.

Energy 502Kcal/2096kJ; Protein 45.8g; Carbohydrate 16.1g, of which sugars 7g; Fat 27g, of which saturates 15g; Cholesterol 220mg; Calcium 249mg; Fibre 2.2g; Sodium 480mg.

CHICKEN AND MUSHROOM PIE

THIS IS A CLASSIC PIE TO BRING A SMILE TO THE FACES OF DINERS OF ALL AGES. PORCINI MUSHROOMS INTENSIFY THE FLAVOUR OF THE CHICKEN AND VEGETABLES UNDER THE MELT-IN-THE-MOUTH CRUST.

SERVES SIX

INGREDIENTS

15g/½oz/¼ cup dried
  porcini mushrooms
50g/2oz/¼ cup butter
30ml/2 tbsp plain (all-purpose) flour
250ml/8fl oz/1 cup hot chicken stock
60ml/4 tbsp single (light) cream
1 onion, coarsely chopped
2 carrots, sliced
2 celery sticks, coarsely chopped
50g/2oz/¾ cup fresh mushrooms,
  quartered
450g/1lb cooked chicken
  meat, cubed
50g/2oz/½ cup fresh or frozen peas
salt and ground black pepper
beaten egg, to glaze

For the pastry
225g/8oz/2 cups plain
  (all-purpose) flour
1.5ml/¼ tsp salt
115g/4oz/½ cup cold butter, diced
65g/2½oz/⅓ cup white vegetable
  fat, diced
60–120ml/4–8 tbsp chilled water

1 To make the pastry, sift the flour and salt into a bowl. Cut or rub in the butter and white vegetable fat until the mixture resembles breadcrumbs. Sprinkle with 90ml/6 tbsp chilled water and mix until the dough holds together. If the dough is too crumbly, add a little more water, 15ml/1 tbsp at a time.

2 Gather the dough into a ball and flatten it into a round. Wrap and chill for at least 30 minutes.

3 To make the filling, put the mushrooms in a bowl. Cover with hot water and soak for 30 minutes. Drain in a muslin- (cheesecloth-) lined sieve (strainer), then dry on kitchen paper. Preheat the oven to 190°C/375°F/Gas 5.

4 Melt half of the butter in a heavy pan. Whisk in the flour and cook until bubbling, whisking constantly. Add the hot stock and whisk over a medium heat until the mixture boils. Cook for 2–3 minutes, then whisk in the cream. Season to taste, and set aside.

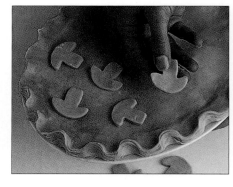

5 Heat the remaining butter in a large, non-stick frying pan and cook the onion and carrots over a low heat for about 5 minutes. Add the celery and fresh mushrooms and cook for 5 minutes more. Stir in the cooked chicken, peas and drained porcini mushrooms.

6 Add the chicken mixture to the hot cream sauce and stir to mix. Adjust the seasoning if necessary. Spoon the mixture into a 2.5 litre/4 pint/2½ quart oval baking dish.

7 Roll out the pastry to a thickness of about 3mm/⅛in. Cut out an oval 2.5cm/1in larger all around than the dish. Lay the pastry over the filling. Gently press around the edge of the dish to seal, then trim off the excess pastry. Crimp the edge of the pastry by pushing the forefinger of one hand into the edge and, using the thumb and forefinger of the other hand, pinch the pastry. Continue all round the pastry edge.

8 Press together the pastry trimmings and roll out again. Cut out mushroom shapes with a sharp knife and stick them on to the pastry lid with beaten egg. Glaze the lid with beaten egg and cut several slits in the pastry to allow the steam to escape.

9 Bake the pie for about 30 minutes, until the pastry has browned. Serve the pie hot.

Energy 576Kcal/2403kJ; Protein 23.8g; Carbohydrate 39.6g, of which sugars 4.7g; Fat 36.9g, of which saturates 20.3g; Cholesterol 127mg; Calcium 104mg; Fibre 3.1g; Sodium 334mg.

LAMB STEW WITH VEGETABLES

THIS FARMHOUSE STEW IS COLOURFUL AND UPLIFTING, WITH LAMB AND YOUNG SPRING VEGETABLES SUCH AS CARROTS, NEW POTATOES, BABY ONIONS, PEAS, FRENCH BEANS AND TURNIPS.

SERVES SIX

INGREDIENTS
60ml/4 tbsp vegetable oil
1.5kg/3–3½lb lamb shoulder,
  trimmed and cut into
  5cm/2in pieces
120ml/4fl oz/½ cup water
45–60ml/3–4 tbsp plain
  (all-purpose) flour
1 litre/1¾ pints/4 cups lamb stock
1 large bouquet garni
3 garlic cloves, lightly crushed
3 ripe tomatoes, skinned, seeded
  and chopped
5ml/1 tsp tomato purée (paste)
675g/1½lb small potatoes, peeled
  or scrubbed
12 baby carrots, scrubbed
115g/4oz French (green) beans, cut
  into 5cm/2in pieces
25g/1 oz/2 tbsp butter
12–18 baby onions
6 medium turnips, quartered
30ml/2 tbsp granulated sugar
¼ tsp dried thyme
175g/6oz/1¼ cups peas
50g/2oz/½ cup mangetouts
  (snow peas)
salt and freshly ground pepper
45ml/3 tbsp chopped fresh parsley or
  coriander (cilantro), to garnish

1 Heat the oil in a large heavy frying pan. Brown the lamb in batches, adding more oil if needed, and place it in a large, flameproof casserole. Add 45ml/ 3 tbsp of the water to the pan and boil for about 1 minute, stirring and scraping the base of the pan, then pour the liquid into the casserole.

2 Sprinkle the flour over the browned meat in the casserole and set it over a medium heat. Cook for 3–5 minutes until browned. Stir in the stock, the bouquet garni, garlic, tomatoes and tomato purée. Season with salt and pepper.

3 Bring to the boil over a high heat. Skim the surface, reduce the heat and simmer, stirring occasionally, for about 1 hour until the meat is tender. Cool the stew to room temperature, cover and chill overnight.

4 About 1½ hours before serving, take the casserole from the refrigerator, lift off the solid fat and blot the surface with kitchen paper to remove all traces of fat. Set the casserole over a medium heat and bring to a simmer. Cook the potatoes in a pan of boiling salted water for 15–20 minutes, then transfer to a bowl and add the carrots to the same water. Cook for 4–5 minutes and transfer to the same bowl. Add the French beans and boil for 2–3 minutes. Transfer to the bowl with the other vegetables.

5 Melt the butter in a heavy frying pan and add the onions and turnips with a further 45ml/3 tbsp water. Cover and cook for 4–5 minutes. Stir in the sugar and thyme and cook until the vegetables are caramelized. Transfer them to the bowl of vegetables. Add the remaining water to the pan. Boil for 1 minute, incorporating the sediment, then add to the lamb.

6 When the lamb and gravy are hot, add the cooked vegetables to the stew and stir gently to distribute. Stir in the peas and mangetouts and cook for 5 minutes until they turn a bright green, then stir in 30ml/2 tbsp of the parsley or coriander.

7 Pour the stew into a large, warmed serving dish. Scatter over the remaining parsley or coriander and serve at once.

VARIATIONS
A wide variety of vegetables can be used in the stew but the trick for success is to avoid overcooking tender young produce. For example, baby broad beans can be added instead of the French beans.
• Young red radishes are delicious instead of, or as well as, the turnips.
• Mint is uplifting and refreshing with the lamb and vegetables – add some instead of the parsley or coriander to garnish, or chop a large handful of fresh mint leaves and add them with the other herbs.

Energy 560Kcal/2346kJ; Protein 39.2g; Carbohydrate 41.9g, of which sugars 14.4g; Fat 27.4g, of which saturates 9.9g; Cholesterol 127mg; Calcium 90mg; Fibre 6.2g; Sodium 181mg.

ROAST LEG OF LAMB

WHEN YOUNG LAMB WAS SEASONAL TO SPRINGTIME, A ROAST LEG WAS AN EASTER SPECIALITY, SERVED WITH A SAUCE USING THE FIRST SPRIGS OF MINT OF THE YEAR AND EARLY NEW POTATOES. ROAST LAMB IS NOW WELL ESTABLISHED AS A YEAR-ROUND FAMILY FAVOURITE FOR SUNDAY LUNCH, OFTEN SERVED WITH CRISP ROAST POTATOES. THE AROMA OF LAMB ROASTING ENLIVENS BOTH APPETITE AND SPIRITS.

SERVES SIX

INGREDIENTS
    1.5kg/3¼lb leg of lamb
    4 garlic cloves, sliced
    2 fresh rosemary sprigs
    30ml/2 tbsp light olive oil
    300ml/½ pint/1¼ cups red wine
    5ml/1 tsp clear honey
    45ml/3 tbsp redcurrant jelly
    salt and ground black pepper
For the roast potatoes
    45ml/3 tbsp white vegetable fat or
      lard (shortening)
    1.3kg/3lb potatoes, such as Desirée,
      cut into chunks
For the mint sauce
    about 15g/½oz/½ cup fresh mint
    10ml/2 tsp caster (superfine) sugar
    15ml/1 tbsp boiling water
    30ml/2 tbsp white wine vinegar

1 Preheat the oven to 220°C/425°F/ Gas 7. Make small slits into the lamb all over the skin. Press a slice of garlic and a few rosemary leaves into each slit, then place the lamb in a roasting pan and season well. Drizzle the oil over the lamb and roast it for about 1 hour, or until it is cooked to taste.

COOK'S TIP
To make a quick and tasty gravy from the pan juices, add about 300ml/½ pint/ 1¼ cups red wine, stock or water and boil, stirring occasionally, until reduced and well-flavoured. Season to taste, then strain into a gravy boat to serve.

2 Meanwhile, mix the wine, honey and redcurrant jelly in a small pan and heat, stirring, until the jelly melts. Bring to the boil, then reduce the heat and simmer until reduced by half. Spoon this glaze over the lamb and return it to the oven for 30–45 minutes.

3 To prepare the potatoes, put the fat in a roasting pan on the oven shelf above the meat. Boil the potatoes for 5–10 minutes, then drain them and fluff up the surface of each with a fork.

4 Add the prepared potatoes to the hot fat and baste well, then roast them for 40–50 minutes, or until they are crisp.

5 Make the mint sauce while the potatoes are roasting. Place the mint on a chopping board and sprinkle the sugar over the top. Chop finely, then transfer the mint and sugar to a bowl.

6 Add the boiling water and stir until the sugar has dissolved. Add 15ml/ 1 tbsp vinegar and taste the sauce before adding the remaining vinegar. You may want to add slightly less or more than the suggested quantity. Leave the mint sauce to stand until you are ready to serve the meal.

7 Cover the lamb with foil and set it aside in a warm place to rest for 10–15 minutes before carving. Serve with the crisp roast potatoes, mint sauce and a selection of seasonal vegetables.

Energy 569Kcal/2376kJ; Protein 51.7g; Carbohydrate 45.2g, of which sugars 10.3g; Fat 35.2g, of which saturates 13.4g; Cholesterol 174mg; Calcium 29mg; Fibre 2.8g; Sodium 130mg.

PORK CASEROLE WITH ONIONS, CHILLI AND DRIED FRUIT

INSPIRED BY SOUTH AMERICAN COOKING, A MOLE — PASTE — OF CHILLI, SHALLOTS AND NUTS IS ADDED TO THIS CASSEROLE OF PORK AND ONIONS. PART OF THE MOLE IS ADDED AT THE END OF COOKING TO RETAIN ITS FRESH FLAVOUR. SERVE WITH RICE AND A GREEN SALAD.

SERVES SIX

INGREDIENTS

- 25ml/1½ tbsp plain (all-purpose) flour
- 1kg/2¼lb shoulder or leg of pork, cut into 5cm/2in cubes
- 45–60ml/3–4 tbsp olive oil
- 2 large onions, chopped
- 2 garlic cloves, finely chopped
- 600ml/1 pint/2½ cups fruity white wine
- 105ml/7 tbsp water
- 115g/4oz ready-to-eat prunes
- 115g/4oz ready-to-eat dried apricots
- grated rind and juice of 1 orange
- pinch of muscovado (molasses) sugar (optional)
- 30ml/2 tbsp chopped fresh parsley
- ½–1 fresh green chilli, seeded and finely chopped (optional)
- salt and ground black pepper

For the mole

- 3 *ancho* chillies and 2 *pasilla* chillies (or other varieties of large, medium-hot dried red chillies)
- 30ml/2 tbsp olive oil
- 2 shallots, chopped
- 2 garlic cloves, chopped
- 1 fresh green chilli, seeded and chopped
- 10ml/2 tsp ground coriander (cilantro)
- 5ml/1 tsp mild Spanish paprika or *pimentón*
- 50g/2oz/½ cup blanched almonds, toasted
- 15ml/1 tbsp chopped fresh oregano or 2.5ml/½ tsp dried oregano

1 Make the mole paste. Toast the chillies in a dry pan over a low heat for 1–2 minutes, until they are aromatic, then soak them in warm water for 30 minutes. Drain, reserving the soaking water, and discard the stalks and seeds.

2 Preheat the oven to 160°C/325°F/Gas 3.

3 Heat the oil in a small frying pan and fry the shallots, garlic, fresh green chilli and ground coriander over a very low heat for 5 minutes.

4 Transfer the shallot mixture to a food processor or blender and add the drained chillies, paprika or *pimentón*, almonds and oregano. Process the mixture, adding 45–60ml/3–4 tbsp of the chilli soaking liquid to make a workable paste.

5 Season the flour with salt and black pepper, then use to coat the pork. Heat 45ml/3 tbsp of the olive oil in a large, heavy frying pan and fry the pork, stirring frequently, until sealed on all sides. Transfer the pork cubes to a flameproof casserole.

6 If necessary, add the remaining oil to the frying pan and cook the onions and garlic gently for 8–10 minutes, stirring occasionally.

7 Add the wine and water to the frying pan. Cook for 2 minutes. Stir in half the mole paste, bring back to the boil and bubble for a few seconds before pouring over the pork.

8 Season lightly with salt and pepper and stir to mix, then cover and cook in the oven for 1½ hours.

9 Increase the oven temperature to 180°C/350°F/Gas 4. Stir in the prunes, apricots and orange juice. Taste the casserole for seasoning, adding the muscovado sugar if necessary, and more salt and pepper. Then cover and cook for another 30–45 minutes until the meat is succulent and delicious.

10 Place the casserole over a direct heat and stir in the remaining mole paste. Simmer, stirring once or twice, for 5 minutes. Serve sprinkled with the orange rind, chopped parsley and fresh chilli, if using.

Energy 468Kcal/1956kJ; Protein 38.8g; Carbohydrate 17.1g, of which sugars 16.9g; Fat 20.7g, of which saturates 4g; Cholesterol 105mg; Calcium 64mg; Fibre 2.9g; Sodium 134mg.

BRAISED PORK CHOPS <u>WITH</u> ONION

THE PIQUANT SAUCE ADDS PUNCH AND FLAVOUR TO THIS SIMPLE SUPPER DISH. SERVE FAVOURITE CREAMY POTATO MASH AND BUTTERY BROCCOLI OR CABBAGE FOR THE PERFECT FEEL-BETTER MEAL.

SERVES FOUR

INGREDIENTS

4 pork loin chops, 2cm/¾in thick
30ml/2 tbsp plain (all-purpose) flour
45ml/3 tbsp olive oil
2 Spanish onions, thinly sliced
2 garlic cloves, finely chopped
250ml/8fl oz/1 cup dry (hard) cider
150ml/¼ pint/⅔ cup vegetable, chicken or pork stock
generous pinch of brown sugar
2 fresh bay leaves
6 fresh thyme sprigs
2 strips lemon rind
120ml/4fl oz/½ cup double (heavy) cream
30–45ml/2–3 tbsp wholegrain mustard
30ml/2 tbsp chopped fresh parsley
salt and ground black pepper

1 Preheat the oven to 200°C/400°F/Gas 6. Trim the chops of excess fat. Season the flour with salt and pepper and use to coat the chops. Heat 30ml/2 tbsp of the oil in a frying pan and brown the chops on both sides, then transfer them to an ovenproof dish.

2 Add the remaining oil to the pan and cook the onions over a fairly gentle heat until they soften and begin to brown at the edges. Add the garlic and cook for 2 minutes more.

3 Stir in any left-over flour, then gradually stir in the cider and stock. Season well with salt and pepper and add the brown sugar, bay leaves, thyme sprigs and lemon rind. Bring the sauce to the boil, stirring constantly, then pour over the chops.

4 Cover and cook in the oven for 20 minutes. Reduce the heat to 180°C/350°F/Gas 4 and continue cooking for another 30–40 minutes. Remove the foil for the last 10 minutes of the cooking time. Remove the chops from the dish and keep warm, covered with foil.

5 Turn the remaining contents of the dish into a pan or, if the dish is flameproof, place it over a direct heat. Discard the herbs and lemon rind, then bring to the boil.

6 Add the cream and continue to boil, stirring constantly. Taste for seasoning, adding a pinch more sugar if necessary. Finally, stir in the mustard to taste and pour the sauce over the braised chops. Sprinkle with the chopped parsley and serve immediately.

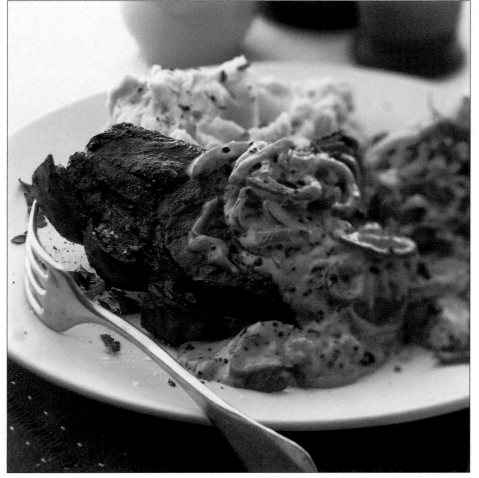

VARIATION
For a less rich sauce, omit the cream and purée the sauce in a blender. Reheat, thinning with a little extra stock if necessary, then adjust the seasoning and add mustard to taste. This will produce a sharper tasting sauce that will need less mustard.

Energy 541Kcal/2253kJ; Protein 39g; Carbohydrate 19.4g, of which sugars 9g; Fat 32.9g, of which saturates 14.1g; Cholesterol 135mg; Calcium 78mg; Fibre 2g; Sodium 88mg.

ROAST PORK WITH SAGE AND ONION STUFFING

SAGE AND ONION STUFFING IS GLORIOUS WITH ROAST PORK AND THERE'S SOMETHING EVER SO CHEERING ABOUT SNEAKING A SAMPLE OF CRACKLING BEFORE SERVING THE MEAT.

SERVES SIX TO EIGHT

INGREDIENTS

1.3–1.6kg/3–3½lb boneless loin of pork
60ml/4 tbsp fine, dry breadcrumbs
10ml/2 tsp chopped fresh sage
25ml/1½ tbsp plain (all-purpose) flour
300ml/½ pint/1¼ cups cider
150ml/¼ pint/⅔ cup water
5–10ml/1–2 tsp crab apple or redcurrant jelly
salt and ground black pepper
sprigs of thyme, to garnish
For the stuffing
25g/1oz/2 tbsp butter
50g/2oz bacon, finely chopped
2 large onions, finely chopped
75g/3oz/1½ cups fresh white breadcrumbs
30ml/2 tbsp chopped fresh sage
5ml/1 tsp chopped fresh thyme
10ml/2 tsp finely grated lemon rind
1 small egg, beaten

1 Preheat the oven to 220°C/425°F/ Gas 7. Make the stuffing first. Melt the butter in a heavy pan and fry the bacon until it begins to brown, then add the onions and cook gently until they soften, but do not allow to brown. Mix with the breadcrumbs, sage, thyme, lemon rind and egg, then season well with salt and pepper.

2 Cut the rind off the joint of pork in one piece and score it well. Cooking the rind separately makes crisper crackling than leaving it on the pork.

3 Place the pork fat-side down and season. Add a layer of stuffing, then roll up and tie neatly.

4 Lay the rind over the pork and rub in 5ml/1 tsp salt. Roast for 2–2½ hours, basting with the pork fat once or twice. Reduce the temperature to 190°C/375ºF/ Gas 5 after 20 minutes. Shape the remaining stuffing into balls and add to the roasting tin for the last 30 minutes.

5 Remove the rind from the pork. Increase the oven temperature to 220°C/425°F/Gas 7 and roast the rind for a further 20–25 minutes, until crisp.

6 Mix the dry breadcrumbs and sage and press them into the fat. Cook the pork for 10 minutes, then cover and set aside in a warm place for 15–20 minutes.

7 Remove all but 30–45ml/2–3 tbsp of the fat from the roasting tin and place it on the hob to make gravy. Stir in the flour, followed by the cider and water. Bring to the boil and then cook gently for 10 minutes. Strain the gravy into a clean pan, add the crab apple or redcurrant jelly, and cook for another 5 minutes. Adjust the seasoning.

8 Serve the pork cut into thick slices and the crisp crackling cut into strips with the cider gravy, garnished with thyme.

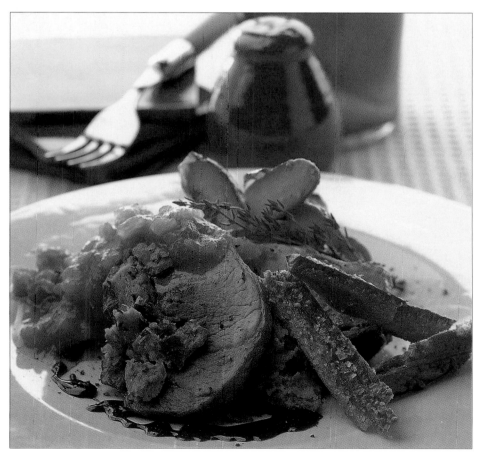

Energy 446Kcal/1874kJ; Protein 52.8g; Carbohydrate 26.4g, of which sugars 5.1g; Fat 15.1g, of which saturates 6g; Cholesterol 185mg; Calcium 76mg; Fibre 1.7g; Sodium 479mg.

CIDER-GLAZED HAM

WHEN THE BLUES STRIKE, FIGHT BACK BY ENTERTAINING RATHER THAN BEING ALONE AND MISERABLE. THERE'S PLENTY OF FABULOUS FLAVOUR AND FOOD VALUE TO SHARE WITH FAMILY AND FRIENDS IN THIS SUBSTANTIAL HAM, PREPARED WITH OLD-FASHIONED ENGLISH INGREDIENTS AND STYLE.

SERVES EIGHT TO TEN

INGREDIENTS

   2kg/4½lb middle gammon (cured
     ham) joint
   1 large or 2 small onions
   about 30 whole cloves
   3 bay leaves
   10 black peppercorns
   1.3 litres/2¼ pints/5⅔ cups medium-
     dry (hard) cider
   45ml/3 tbsp soft light brown sugar
   bunch of flat leaf parsley, to garnish
For the cranberry sauce
   350g/12oz/3 cups cranberries
   175g/6oz/¾ cup soft light brown sugar
   grated rind and juice of
     2 clementines
   30ml/2 tbsp port

1 Weigh the gammon and calculate the cooking time at 20 minutes per 450g/1lb, then place it in a large flameproof casserole or pan. Stud the onion or onions with 5–10 of the cloves and add to the casserole or pan with the bay leaves and peppercorns. (A large stockpot is ideal for cooking a big piece of meat but a deep roasting tin or pan will do in an emergency, with foil as a cover and turning the meat often for even cooking.)

2 Add 1.2 litres/2 pints/5 cups of the cider and enough water just to cover the gammon. Heat until simmering and then carefully skim off the scum that rises to the surface using a large spoon or ladle. Start timing the cooking from the moment the stock begins to simmer.

3 Cover with a lid or foil and simmer gently for the calculated time. Towards the end of the cooking time, preheat the oven to 220°C/425°F/Gas 7.

4 Heat the sugar and remaining cider in a pan; stir until the sugar has dissolved.

5 Simmer for 5 minutes to make a dark, sticky glaze. Remove the pan from the heat and leave to cool for 5 minutes.

6 Lift the gammon out of the casserole or pan. Carefully and evenly, cut the rind from the meat, then score the fat into a diamond pattern. Place the gammon in a large roasting pan or ovenproof dish.

7 Press a clove into the centre of each diamond, then carefully spoon over the glaze. Bake for 20–25 minutes, or until the fat is brown, glistening and crisp.

8 To make the cranberry sauce, simmer all the ingredients in a heavy pan for 15–20 minutes, stirring frequently. Transfer the sauce to a jug (pitcher). Serve the gammon hot or cold, garnished with parsley and with the cranberry sauce.

COOK'S TIP

Leave the gammon until it is just cool enough to handle before removing the rind. Snip off the string using a sharp knife or scissors, then carefully slice off the rind, leaving a thin, even layer of fat. Use a narrow-bladed, sharp knife for the best results.

VARIATION

Use honey in place of the soft light brown sugar for the glaze and serve the meat with redcurrant sauce or jelly.

Energy 447Kcal/1873kJ; Protein 44.1g; Carbohydrate 25.6g, of which sugars 25.6g; Fat 18.8g, of which saturates 6.3g; Cholesterol 58mg; Calcium 35mg; Fibre 1.3g; Sodium 2203mg.

STEAK <u>AND</u> KIDNEY PIE <u>WITH</u> MUSTARD GRAVY

FRAGRANT MUSTARD, BAY AND PARSLEY GRAVY COMPLEMENTS THE BEEF BEAUTIFULLY IN THIS FABULOUS PIE THAT IS A PLEASURE TO PREPARE AS WELL AS TO EAT — A DEFINITE SPIRIT-LIFTER.

SERVES FOUR

INGREDIENTS

450g/1lb puff pastry
40ml/2½ tbsp plain
  (all-purpose) flour
675g/1½lb rump (round)
  steak, cubed
175g/6oz lamb's kidneys
25g/1oz/2 tbsp butter
1 onion, chopped
15ml/1 tbsp English (hot) mustard
2 bay leaves
15ml/1 tbsp chopped fresh parsley
150ml/¼ pint/⅔ cup beef stock
1 egg, beaten
salt and ground black pepper

1 Roll out two-thirds of the pastry on a floured surface to a thickness of 3mm/⅛in. Use to line the base and sides of a 1.5 litre/2½ pint/6¼ cup pie dish. Place a pie funnel in the centre of the dish.

2 Put the flour, salt and pepper in a bowl and toss the steak in the mixture.

3 Remove the fat, skin and tough central core from the kidneys, and slice them thickly. Add the slices to the steak and toss well.

4 Melt the butter in a pan, add the onion and fry over a low heat, stirring occasionally, until soft and translucent. Add the mustard, bay leaves, parsley and stock and stir well.

5 Preheat the oven to 190°C/375°F/ Gas 5. Place the steak and kidney in the pie dish and add the stock mixture.

6 Roll out the remaining puff pastry to a thickness of 3mm/⅛in to use for the pie lid. Brush the edges of the pastry case with beaten egg and cover with the lid. Press the edges firmly together to seal, then trim. Use the trimmings to decorate the top with pastry leaves.

7 Brush the pie with a little beaten egg and make a small hole in the pastry lid for the funnel. Bake for about 1 hour until the pastry is well risen and golden brown. Serve the pie hot, straight from the pie dish.

Energy 773Kcal/3238kJ; Protein 52.7g; Carbohydrate 54.3g, of which sugars 3.8g; Fat 41g, of which saturates 6.6g; Cholesterol 251mg; Calcium 104mg; Fibre 0.9g; Sodium 555mg.

BOEUF BOURGUIGNONNE

THE CLASSIC FRENCH DISH OF BEEF PREPARED IN BURGUNDY STYLE, WITH RED WINE, SMALL PIECES OF BACON, SHALLOTS AND MUSHROOMS, IS COOKED FOR SEVERAL HOURS AT A LOW TEMPERATURE.

SERVES SIX

INGREDIENTS

175g/6oz rindless streaky (fatty)
   bacon rashers (strips), chopped
900g/2lb lean braising steak, such
   as top rump (rump roast) of beef or
   braising steak
30ml/2 tbsp plain (all-purpose) flour
45ml/3 tbsp sunflower oil
25g/1oz/2 tbsp butter
12 shallots
2 garlic cloves, crushed
175g/6oz/2⅓ cups mushrooms, sliced
450ml/¾ pint/scant 2 cups robust
   red wine
150ml/¼ pint/⅔ cup beef stock
   or consommé
1 bay leaf
2 sprigs each of fresh thyme, parsley
   and marjoram
salt and ground black pepper

1 Preheat the oven to 160°C/325°F/ Gas 3. Heat a large flameproof casserole, then add the bacon and cook, stirring occasionally, until the pieces are crisp and golden brown.

2 Meanwhile, cut the meat into 2.5cm/ 1in cubes. Season the flour and use to coat the meat. Use a slotted spoon to remove the bacon from the casserole and set aside. Add and heat the oil, then brown the beef in batches and set aside with the bacon.

VARIATION
Use lardons, which are available from large supermarkets, instead of the bacon.

3 Add the butter to the fat remaining in the casserole. Cook the shallots and garlic until just starting to colour, then add the mushrooms and cook for a further 5 minutes. Replace the bacon and meat, and stir in the wine and stock or consommé. Tie the bay leaf, thyme, parsley and marjoram together into a bouquet garni and add to the casserole.

4 Cover and cook in the oven for 1½ hours, or until the meat is tender, stirring once or twice. Season to taste and serve the casserole with creamy mashed root vegetables, such as celeriac and potatoes.

COOK'S TIP
Boeuf Bourguignonne freezes very well. Transfer the mixture to a dish so that it cools quickly, then pour it into a rigid plastic container. Push all the cubes of meat down into the sauce or they will dry out. Freeze for up to 2 months. Thaw overnight in the refrigerator, then transfer to a flameproof casserole and add 150ml/¼ pint/⅔ cup water. Stir well, bring to the boil, stirring occasionally, and simmer steadily for at least 10 minutes, or until the meat is hot.

Energy 455Kcal/1898kJ; Protein 39.2g; Carbohydrate 6.9g, of which sugars 1.7g; Fat 24.7g, of which saturates 8.9g; Cholesterol 122mg; Calcium 36mg; Fibre 1.1g; Sodium 500mg.

STEAK WITH STOUT AND POTATOES

THE IRISH WAY TO BRAISE BEEF IS IN STOUT OF COURSE AND TOPPED WITH THICKLY SLICED POTATOES. BAKE IT IN A MEDIUM OVEN FOR LONG, SLOW TENDERIZING IF YOU PREFER.

SERVES FOUR

INGREDIENTS
675g/1½lb stewing beef
15ml/1 tbsp vegetable oil
25g/1oz/2 tbsp butter
225g/8oz tiny white onions
175ml/6fl oz/¾ cup stout or dark beer
300ml/½ pint/1¼ cups beef stock
bouquet garni
675g/1½lb firm, waxy potatoes, cut into thick slices
225g/8oz/3 cups large mushrooms, sliced
15ml/1 tbsp plain (all-purpose) flour
2.5ml/½ tsp mild mustard
salt and ground black pepper
chopped thyme sprigs, to garnish

3 Add the tiny white onions to the pan and cook for 3–4 minutes until lightly browned all over. Return the steak to the pan with the onions. Pour on the stout or beer and stock and season the whole mixture to taste.

5 Add the sliced mushrooms over the potatoes. Cover again and simmer for a further 30 minutes or so. Remove the steak and vegetables with a slotted spoon and arrange on a platter.

1 Trim any excess fat from the steak and cut into four pieces. Season both sides of the meat. Heat the oil and 10g/¼oz/1½ tsp of the butter in a large heavy pan.

4 Next add the bouquet garni to the pan and top with the potato slices distributing them evenly over the surface to cover the steak. Bring the ingredients to a boil then reduce the heat, cover with a tight-fitting lid and simmer gently for 1 hour.

6 Mix the remaining butter with the flour to make a roux. Whisk a little at a time into the cooking liquid in the pan. Stir in the mustard. Cook over a medium heat for 2–3 minutes, stirring all the while, until thickened.

7 Season the sauce and pour over the steak. Garnish with plenty of thyme sprigs and serve the dish at once.

2 Add the steak and brown on both sides, taking care not to burn the butter. Remove from the pan and set aside.

COOK'S TIP
To make onion peeling easier, first put the onions in a bowl and cover with boiling water. Allow them to soak for about 5 minutes and drain. The skins should now peel away easily.

VARIATION
For a dish that is lighter, but just as tasty, substitute four lamb leg steaks for the beef, and use dry (hard) cider instead of the stout or beer, and lamb or chicken stock instead of beef.

Energy 468Kcal/1968kJ; Protein 43.4g; Carbohydrate 38.9g, of which sugars 8.7g; Fat 14.8g, of which saturates 6.2g; Cholesterol 126mg; Calcium 50mg; Fibre 3.3g; Sodium 195mg.

TRADITIONAL BEEF STEW AND DUMPLINGS

THIS DISH CAN COOK IN THE OVEN WHILE YOU GO FOR A LONG WALK TO WORK UP AN APPETITE.

SERVES SIX

INGREDIENTS
25g/1oz/1 tbsp plain (all-purpose)
   flour
1.2kg/2½lb stewing steak, cubed
30ml/2 tbsp olive oil
2 large onions, sliced
450g/1lb carrots, sliced
300ml/½ pint/1¼ cups stout
   or dark beer
3 bay leaves
10ml/2 tsp brown sugar
3 fresh thyme sprigs
5ml/1 tsp cider vinegar
salt and freshly ground black pepper
For the dumplings
115g/4oz/1½ cups grated hard
   white fat
225g/8oz/2 cups self-raising (self-
   rising) flour
30ml/2 tbsp chopped mixed
   fresh herbs
about 150ml/¼ pint/⅔ cup water

1 Preheat the oven to 160°C/325°F/
Gas 3. Season the flour and sprinkle
over the meat, tossing to coat.

2 Heat the oil in large casserole and
lightly sauté the onions and carrots.
Remove the vegetables with a slotted
spoon and reserve them.

3 Brown the meat well in batches in
the casserole.

4 Return all the vegetables to the
casserole and add any leftover
seasoned flour. Add the stout or beer,
bay leaves, sugar and thyme. Bring the
liquid to the boil, cover and then
transfer to the oven. Leave the meat to
cook for 1 hour and 40 minutes, before
making the dumplings.

5 Mix the grated fat, flour and herbs
together. Add enough water to make a
soft sticky dough.

6 Form the dough into small balls with
floured hands. Add the cider vinegar to
the meat and spoon the dumplings on
top. Cook for a further 20 minutes, until
the dumplings have cooked through,
and serve hot.

COOK'S TIPS
Suet pastry is one of the easiest pastries
to make. Remember always to use self-
raising flour for a light and fluffy result.
Traditionally, shredded beef suet is used
but vegetable suet is also available.
Alternatively, as in this recipe, white
cooking fat can be coarsely grated and
used. Thoroughly chill the fat, placing it
in the freezer for 10 minutes if
necessary, and chill the grater. This way
the fat will not melt as it is grated.
Then, when mixing and shaping the
pastry, handle it as lightly as possible
and avoid over-mixing. When cooked
uncovered, the dough turns golden
brown and slightly crusty on the
surface. When covered, it is soft, white
and fluffy. If the casserole is not big
enough to hold the stew and dumplings,
the dumplings can be simmered in a
pan of stock or water for about 15
minutes, until risen and fluffy. Drain
well on a slotted spoon and place on
top of the meat or on the plates.

Energy 648Kcal/2714kJ; Protein 50.3g; Carbohydrate 42.9g, of which sugars 10.6g; Fat 30.5g, of which saturates 11.2g; Cholesterol 152mg; Calcium 184mg; Fibre 4g; Sodium 297mg.

ROAST RIB OF BEEF

THIS BEATS ALL OTHER CUTS ON FLAVOUR. WITH YORKSHIRE PUDDINGS AND HORSERADISH SAUCE, IT IS IDEAL FOR A SUNDAY LUNCH GATHERING. WHAT BETTER WAY TO JOLLY UP A DISMAL WINTRY WEEK?

SERVES EIGHT TO TEN

INGREDIENTS
- 45ml/3 tbsp mixed peppercorns
- 15ml/1 tbsp juniper berries
- 2.75kg/6lb rolled rib of beef
- 30ml/2 tbsp Dijon mustard
- 15ml/1 tbsp olive oil

For the Yorkshire puddings
- 150ml/¼ pint/⅔ cup water
- 150ml/¼ pint/⅔ cup milk
- 115g/4oz/1 cup plain
  (all-purpose) flour
- pinch of salt
- 2 eggs, beaten
- 60ml/4 tbsp lard (shortening),
  melted, or sunflower oil (optional)

For the caramelized shallots
- 20 shallots
- 5 garlic cloves, peeled
- 60ml/4 tbsp light olive oil
- 15ml/1 tbsp caster (superfine) sugar

For the gravy
- 150ml/¼ pint/⅔ cup red wine
- 600ml/1 pint/2½ cups beef stock
- salt and ground black pepper

1 Preheat the oven to 230°C/450°F/ Gas 8. Crush the peppercorns and juniper berries. Sprinkle half the spices over the meat. Transfer to a roasting pan and roast for 30 minutes.

COOK'S TIP
If you prefer to cook beef on the bone, buy a 3.6kg/8lb forerib. Trim off the excess fat, scatter over the spices, then follow the instructions in steps 1 and 2. Roast at the lower temperature for 2 hours for rare beef, 2½ hours for medium rare, and 3 hours for well done.

2 Reduce the oven temperature to 180°C/350°F/Gas 4. Mix the mustard and oil into the remaining crushed spices and spread the resulting paste over the meat. Roast the meat for a further 1¼ hours if you like your meat rare, 1 hour 50 minutes for a medium-rare result or 2 hours 25 minutes for a joint that is medium to well done. Baste the joint frequently during cooking.

3 Make the Yorkshire puddings as soon as the beef is in the oven. Stir the water into the milk. Sift the flour and salt into a bowl. Make a well in the middle and gradually whisk in the eggs, followed by the milk and water to make a smooth batter. Cover and leave to stand for about 1 hour. (The batter can be made well in advance and chilled overnight in the refrigerator if convenient.)

4 An hour before the beef is due to be ready, mix the shallots and garlic cloves with the light olive oil and spoon into the roasting pan around the beef. After about 30 minutes, lightly sprinkle the sugar over the shallots and garlic, and stir the shallots and garlic 2–3 times during cooking.

5 Transfer the meat to a serving platter, cover tightly with foil and set aside in a warm place for 20–30 minutes. (This resting time makes carving easier.) Increase the oven temperature to 230°C/450°F/Gas 8. Divide 60ml/4 tbsp dripping from the meat or the lard or oil, if using, among 10 individual Yorkshire pudding pans or 16 large patty tins (muffin pans), and heat in the oven for about 5 minutes.

6 Spoon the Yorkshire pudding batter into the hot fat in the tins and bake for 20–30 minutes, or until risen, firm and golden brown. The time depends on the size of the tins: larger Yorkshire puddings will take longer than those in patty tins.

7 Make the gravy while the Yorkshire puddings are cooking. Simmer the red wine and beef stock together in a pan for about 5 minutes to intensify the flavour of the gravy.

8 Skim the fat from the meat juices in the roasting pan, then pour in the wine mixture and simmer until the gravy is reduced and thickened slightly to a syrupy consistency. Stir frequently with a wooden spoon to remove all of the roasting residue from the roasting pan. Season to taste.

9 Serve the beef with the individual Yorkshire puddings, caramelized shallots and gravy. Offer roast potatoes or game chips as accompaniments along with a selection of lightly cooked, seasonal vegetables.

Energy 741Kcal/3098kJ; Protein 78.5g; Carbohydrate 13.5g, of which sugars 2.6g; Fat 40.5g, of which saturates 15.8g; Cholesterol 245mg; Calcium 83mg; Fibre 1.1g; Sodium 216mg.

INDEX

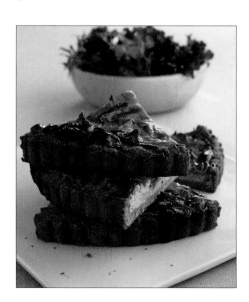

ACKNOWLEDGEMENTS

Recipes: Catherine Atkinson, Mary Banks, Alex Barker, Judy Bastyra, Angela Boggiano, Maxine Clark, Roz Denny, Joanna Farrow, Jennie Fleetwood, Brian Glover, Nicola Graimes, Deh-Ta Hsiung, Christine Ingram, Becky Johnson, Lucy Knox, Sally Mansfield, Christine McFadden, Jane Milton, Sallie Morris, Keith Richmond, Jennie Shapter, Marlena Spieler, Liz Trigg, Jenny White, Kate Whiteman, Lucy Whiteman, Jeni Wright.

Home economists: Eliza Baird, Alex Barker, Caroline Barty, Joanna Farrow, Annabel Ford, Christine France, Carole Handslip, Kate Jay, Becky Johnson, Jill Jones, Bridget Sargeson, Jennie Shapter, Carol Tennant, Sunil Vijayakar, Jenny White.

Stylists: Nicki Dowey, Penny Markham, Lucy McKelvie, Marion Price, Helen Trent, Linda Tubby.

Photographers: Frank Adam, Tim Auty, Martin Brigdale, Louisa Dare, Nicki Dowey, Gus Filgate, John Heseltine, Amanda Heywood, Janine Hosegood, Dave King, William Lingwood, Thomas Odulate, Craig Robertson, Simon Smith, Sam Stowell.